AF497622

MEETING THE UNIVERSE

MEETING THE UNIVERSE

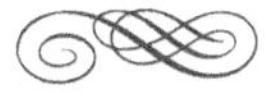

*The journey of
my soul*

NIKO RIKI

Copyright © 2022 by Niko Riki

All rights reserved. This book or any portion thereof may not be reproduced or used in any manner whatsoever without the express written permission of the publisher except for the use of brief quotations in a book review.

Some characters an events in this book are fictitious. Any similarity to real persons, living or dead, is coincidental and not intended by the author.

Printed in the United States of America
kronbergmeggy@gmail.com

First Printing, 2022

ISBN 978-3-9824382-0-7

CONTENTS

I

Mother's mysterious disappearance

Vincent's first vivid childhood memories had flown with the wings of the wind, and they began to speak to him in a loud voice. He began to sink into them like quicksand. The glass of brandy slipped out of his hands, just as he had decided to pour himself a bit more of the alcohol, and shattered into many tiny shards with a loud bang.

- Maybe it's a warning that I must change my life? - Vincent thought but, the painful childhood memories became brighter and more robust than the golden brandy he had drunk.

Vincent laid heavy on the wooden floor, closed his eyes, and plunged into the whirlpool of childhood memories. In front of his eyes, his hometown, located on a steep hill next to an eternally chattering river, appeared as a bright painting.

- Get away from me! – his mother's words cut into his heart like a knife.

Vincent was just six years old when he packed his tiger backpack with his blue jacket, beloved plush teddy bear, and a candy box. He was ready for his first big independent step.

- I'm leaving now, mom! Okay?

Mother looked at him and asked:

- Where are you going?

- I'm just going to keep walking forward! - the little boy said quietly.

- No, stay here, don't go anywhere! - my mother said strictly with tears in her eyes.

It was the first unpleasant argument with his mother when the child thought that maybe his mom didn't love him at all. The feeling of rejection had penetrated so deep into Vincent's heart that he seemed to be superfluous in this world. All the little boy had wanted was to give his mother a gift. Vincent had put mud in his mother's winter shoes and had planted two large velvets in them, which a flower stall seller had given to Vincent because he had come into the store with a huge smile and said Hello. Vincent took off his boots, placed his bag on the rocking chair in the corner of the room, rushed to the bed, and began to cry.

- Why doesn't she love me?

Tears were bursting like heavy raindrops and made the feather-stuffed pillow moistened, which he had received as a gift from an unfamiliar man in glasses that his mother once treated to a cup of coffee.

* * *

- Wake up! It's time to go to kindergarten - Mom shook his shoulder.

He opened his sleepy eyes, which were stuck together as if glued shut, and saw his mother's smiling face. A warm drop of honey poured into his heart, the small birds were chatting outside the window and knocked on the pane as if greeting:

- Good morning, little boy!

Vincent ran into the bathroom and looked in the mirror. With his little hands, he took one strand of his curly golden hair, pulled it down, and let it go, while it playfully bounced back like the most flexible spring. The boy tried to scrub his freckles off with a bath sponge but, when his skin turned red, he put it back on the locker and winked at his reflection in the round mirror with his dark blue eyes.

- Children, I've given you a piece of paper and colored pencils, now your job is to draw your family, - the teacher explained loudly.

Looking around at the drawings of the other children, the question arose. Why do other children draw a man next to their moms? The fact that there are sisters and brothers, I know that but, I do not understand what a father is.

- Why do you have an empty page? Why don't you draw anything?

- I don't have a family!

- You don't have a family? But mom comes to pick you up!

- Do Mom, and I count as family? There are only two of us but, don't other children have a third person?

- Of course, it counts! - the teacher raised her eyebrows in shock and tapped on his shoulder.

Vincent sighed with relief and drew himself and his beloved mummy but finished the drawing by wrapping a large red heart around them and a yellow sun in the corner of the page with as many rays as possible.

While Vincent was looking at the other children, he felt a slight ache because more than anything else, he wished he had a father who could lift him on his shoulders, then he would be as big as all adults, and no one would call him a boy anymore.

One of the kindergarten boys, Nikolai, told Vincent about events with his father and how they spend time together, the games they play, cars and dinosaurs' figurines they collect, and the football they play together. This guy had everything; he had a father, a mother, and a brother! If he wanted some toy, then his father always bought it.

Vincent turned his back to Nikolai and left him to play with Legos because he didn't want to listen to this bragging anymore. He pulled a plastic box marked with a colorful rainbow ball out of the small locker his mother had bought. He touched every piece of oblong plastic with his little fingers and chose to pick up the blue color, and began rolling it hard in his tiny hands. He took the red, blue, and black colors until the plastic bricks mixed into one large ball.

- What a beautiful planet! - the teacher was surprised.

Vincent, too, enjoyed the colorful formation and plunged into a flurry of questions. What is a planet? And how did it come to be? How is it possible that Earth is round, and people walk on it without falling off?

- Vincent, let's learn letters! - Alexander spoke up.

- Do you know the alphabet?

- My sister taught me the alphabet.

Alexander pointed to the white notebooks lying on the shelf, took one of them, and invited him to sit in the corner of the room on the small bench. The dark-haired guy drew a line, then another, and finally the third. Vincent looked closely at what these miraculous lines would turn into.

- It's the letter A, - Alexander nodded and rolled his brown eyes just at the moment when tall Linda pulled a notebook out of his hands with lightning speed. She punched his side and, together with her friends, started to scribble on those pages.

How unfair, we want to learn how to write letters but, that terrible Linda punches for no reason and grabs the notebook, preventing us from learning.

- We need to tell that to our teacher, - Vincent said angrily.

- There's no point! - Alexander sighed and silently walked to the wooden brick box, building something resembling a crooked tower.

- What audacity! How can you do that! - outraged, the teacher ran out of the dressing room.

- What happened? - The nanny asked in shock.

- I wanted to run to the group next door quickly but, I saw Linda put my lipstick in her pocket! You can't do that! - the teacher growled and put pink boots on little Anna's feet while their fluffy balls hit each other and resembled a snowflake dance as the girl moved.

- Get dressed! - the nanny commanded and opened the heavy entrance door', which was so big that children could reach its wiggly floral-patterned handle only when standing on tiptoes. If one of the children tried to reach it, the nanny always got angry, and her face turned into a red hue.

- Look how beautiful snowflakes fall from the sky; they spin, dance, and melt in my glove! Vincent erupted with a happy smile.

- It's a shame that such beauty is melting but, the man in the sky just shakes his big bag, and many other little snow-flakes descend from the sky, - thought the little boy and waited for them to fly into his mouth as he stuck out his tongue.

- Look at these beautiful icicles, - said the boastful Nicho-las and raised his hand towards the largest one, - Behold, this icicle is mine! -

Vincent looked at the vast icicles and thought how beau-tiful they were when he looked through them. Other children seemed tiny, and there were water bubbles inside that could be seen but could not be felt by hand.

- It's a miracle, this icicle! Please give it to me! - the curly boy called in delight.

- No, it's mine; I chose it first!

- All right, take my dragon chain! - Vincent pulled the chain over his head that his mother had given him and thought she would like this icicle much better. She would love her special gift.

- Hmm but, what I'm going to tell her about the dragon chain? She told me not to lose it, - thought the boy.

Vincent squeezed the chain into Nicholas' patterned mitten and broke off the giant icicle. He put it in his jacket, and although the icicle was rather significant, it still fit into the oblong pocket.

- Mommy will surely love my gift! She will be in a good mood when she sees the miracle, I've prepared for her, - the blue-eyed boy whispered. He waited for mommy until she finally came to pick him up from the kindergarten. He was the last one left in the group with a kindergarten teacher.

- I'm so sorry, got held up at work! - Vincent's mother rushed in and smelled of fresh winter air.

- Mom, finally you're here. Where were you for so long?

- I had a lot of work to do.

- Teacher, my mom is a strong woman because she works in a factory!

The teacher smiled and nodded vigorously at the little family.

- The first one to bring the child in the morning and the last one to pick him up! - thought the teacher, who hurriedly headed home.

- Mom, look, I've got you a winter present! - the little boy grabbed the broken icicle but instead saw that it had melted altogether.

To his surprise, when they returned home and entered the large room, the previously met man, who had given the teal pillow, was sitting on the couch. The boy pulled the sizeable blue folders from underneath the sofa and showed his drawings to the strange guest while he was drinking orange juice. Vincent had drawn when it was raining outside or when his best friend Alexander did not come to play in the yard.

The man watched the drawings with great interest and complimented him variously about the awkward characters. When the bearded man had drunk some coffee and had eaten the honey cake, he wanted to leave but, Vincent's mother stopped him and spat out in anger:

- Where's the help from you?

The man looked at his mother's angered eyes and quietly said that he didn't have money and slowly walked out the door into the dark corridor of the house.

- Mom, who is this man?

- It's your dad! - Mom said and went to the kitchen.

- Dad??? - Vincent couldn't believe that he had a father.

- But if so, why don't they live together, and it looks like my mom hates him so much? - the little boy thought.

A dark shadow crossed mother's pale face, and deep pain and a sense of frustration became apparent in her eyes. She turned towards the kitchen door and went to the old dresser, one leg of which had been broken off, and swung lightly in the wind. She opened the dresser and stared at it for a long time as if she couldn't understand what she was looking for.

- Mom, where are you going? - the little boy asked with his eyes wide in shock.

- Stay in the room! I'm sick of all this! - Mom said and closed the door.

Thinking his mother was in a bad mood, the boy didn't take his mother's sharp tone to heart and crawled under a wooden chair to play with a tin soldier.

It was getting dark outside but, mom didn't seem to care about little Vincent. The boy walked up to the room door, stood on his toes, and tried to reach the metal door handle but, no matter how hard he tried, the little boy couldn't get it, then he figured he could step on the little wooden bench under the bed. He could reach the door handle this time, and the heavy door slowly opened with a squeaky sound.

- Mom, I want to eat! - With quick steps, Vincent ran into the kitchen and looked for where his mother was gone but, she wasn't there. His heart started beating faster, and the boy started looking for his mom all over the house but, she was lost; she wasn't in the bathroom, the basement, or the back-yard. Vincent frowned in confusion, and two large droplets of tears flowed his cheeks.

- Mommy! Mommy! Mom! - Vincent called out in despair and ran from the overgrown yard to the back of the house, looking through all the possible rooms, he was looking even in the tiny kitchen dresser and behind the bed but, no matter how many times he looked, and how many times he searched, the little boy didn't find his mother. He knelt and started crying, curled up in a ball, he lay down on a mat that was slightly bigger than the little boy himself, and his eyelids got heavier and heavier to greet the coming sleep...

* * *

The sun outside the window began to warm Vincent's face, and the little boy slowly opened his sleep-clumped eyes; this time, he had slept on the cold floor instead of the soft crib next to his toy tiger. A tin soldier slipped out of his hand but, the little boy didn't even notice it because he realized that yesterday's events had been not an unpleasant nightmare but a reality.

- Knock! Knock! Knock! - the little boy's fright was interrupted by hollow knocks on the door.

- Mom, is that you? - Vincent asked in a shaky voice.

- Good morning, this is the police! Open the door, please! - a man spat in a hollow voice.

Vincent went after the wooden bench, stepped on it, pulled the big metal key out of his trouser pocket with trembling hands, and put it in the lock.

As the heavy wooden door slowly opened, the boy instantly saw three pairs of legs.

- Mom's not home! - the boy said and tried to close the door but, before he could fully close it, the man who had previously addressed Vincent in a door gap stopped the door and said.

- Are you Vincent?

- Yes, my name is Vincent! What do you want from me? My Mom is not home!

You must bring your belongings and come with us! - said the woman in the white jacket and perfectly ironed trousers, which had no wrinkles or creases. She was holding a thick black folder in her hands.

The man, dressed in police uniform, opened the door wider, and all three visitors entered the old wooden house. A woman with a thick folder diligently began to look at the ceiling and walked around the entire house, the floor clattered loudly from her high heels, and in some places, the boards swayed.

A second woman approached the boy and gently put her hand on his shoulder:

- It's time to pack up! It's going to be all right, don't worry, - smiled the woman and opened the closet in the corner of the room, and started to put the boy's clothes in the bag.

- I'm not going anywhere; I must wait for my mom! - said Vincent and watched with his mouth wide.

A woman wearing the white suit, saying nothing, carried Vincent's bag of clothes to the police car and approached the little boy with a quick pace, and said as she grabbed his hand:

- Your mom's gone; now other good people will take care of you.

- Where's she gone??? - the boy asked in surprise.

- To your relatives! - the policeman determined and picked up the little boy in his arms and carried him to the car; it didn't even help that Vincent kicked and punched the stocky man in his arms.

- No, don't take me away; I haven't done anything wrong! I want my mom! - with his tiny fists punching, the boy called desperately against the man's chest.

- Calm down! You'll be better off there! There will be other children! - the man said and pushed the boy into a police car. The first thing Vincent decided to do was open the car's door. He grabbed the car handle and opened the door; the large man, noticing it, became very nervous and, as if he was shot with an electric current, jumped out of the driver's seat and quickly slammed the door through which the boy threw wanted to getaway.

- You're not getting out this time! - the man said and locked the door.

Vincent tried to get out of the car repeatedly to escape this unknown.

- How do adults imagine that they have power over children? Just because they're bigger doesn't mean they can take me somewhere against my will. Don't they understand that I have to be home and wait for my mom to return from the trip? When she comes back, how will she know where I am? What if I disappear now, just as my mom disappeared? And I don't want to go to another place where there are other kids; I'm okay with my mom alone.

How long will my mom be away? Has something maybe happened to her? - A flurry of questions flew into little Vincent's mind, - Please don't hurt me! Take me back home because I have to wait for my mom. She'll be back soon.

- When she'll be back, she'll come and pick you up, and we'll tell her where you are, - the man sighed heavily and looked a little bit sad at the little boy in the rear-view mirror. Vincent heard the wheels of the car move and slowly moved away towards the rocky road as the mud splashed off the porch of the house. The boy watched as the wooden hut grew smaller and smaller until it disappeared entirely behind the thick spruce branches.

As he passed the bus stop, Vincent watched as a man with a green bottle in his hands was lying on a bench, and another man was lying nearby in the green grass.

- What an unusual place to sleep! Why don't they sleep in their homes but on the street? How strange people can sometimes be, as if grown-up but, behave so foolishly, - the boy thought and nudged the glass of the car with his finger, on which the thumbprint in the form of a crescent appeared.

The old brick bridge caught Vincent's eyes, the place he often came together with his mom. At the shores of the small stream, the boy used to train in stone skipping; for now, his best record was three skips but, the boy from the kindergarten said that he could do thirty skips.

As he passed the old bridge, the boy stared into the unseen expansive countryside, the middling branches of trees, and hoped to see a hidden forest doe or bunny behind bushes or thick branches.

The driver pulled up to a white three-floor building and said:

- We're here!

2

The Presence of unconcern

- Knock! Knock! Knock! - the loud knocks rang in her head as if to say that they shall not be forgotten about.

She clutched her head and fell to her knees, pushing aside the bloody red curtains with her trembling hands. In the reflection of the window, a monster-like face started moving and was looking right through her with its glowing, fiery eyes, as if it wanted to swallow her whole and leave not one bone behind.

Vincent's mother tried to scream but could not, as the fear had wholly paralyzed her. Her heart was beating so fast; it seemed like it would come to the point of stopping very soon.

The massive wooden door opened, squeaking loudly and

bouncing off the white wall with a rumble of drums, and the strange, unfamiliar noise could be heard.

- Are you here??? Are you here??? I am coming for you! - the voice came closer and closer.

- Noooo! - the woman whispered in a quiet and trembling voice. She could not bear to look to the door side, from where the strange voice came.

She felt the steps becoming louder and louder; the fast-paced walk came closer and closer to her, along with the squeaking of wooden plates. She felt how a cold arm put its hands on her shoulder.

Vincent's mother listened to her heartbeats, which were so loudly and mightily, and started to breathe heavily and felt short of breath. She closed her eyes and stuffed her ears with her fingertips, hoping that the morning would soon come and the sun would rise and everything would be okay again but, the voice didn't stop but instead became even louder.

- I am here! You can't escape from me! - the voice shouted in a commanding tone.

- God, Heavenly Father, your almighty name... - the woman quietly started praying and, at the same time, questioned whether she should or shouldn't take a peek.

- Stop being such a coward! - her inner voice said.

She slowly turned her head to face the voice and noticed nobody around as she opened her eyes. Relieved, she breathed out and got back up on her feet, ready to go to bed but, then she noticed that, in the corridor, a dark figure seemed to be moving and knocking on the windowpane. She immediately froze as if she had turned into a large stone.

- Where are you going to run? You have nowhere to run to, don't you? - the low voice of a strange man repeated, although, this time, it sounded different from the voice she had heard before.

- Go away! - the woman said without conviction.

- You have nowhere to run to! - the voice repeated itself, knocking at the windowpane. She came closer to the window and saw the same monster silhouette that she had seen earlier.

- I cannot stay here anymore!!! - the woman grabbed her puffy leather jacket that had fallen to the floor near the armchair and, just like heavy wind, stormed out of the room with her eyes closed. She was running straight at the silhouette that stood in the corridor without moving, her whole body was trembling, and she felt cold cramps all over her body. Her umbrella fell to the floor and touched her leg.

- Go on, run, you fool! - the tall figure croaked, laughing loudly.

She stuffed her ears, trying to find the doorknob with her elbow but, it seemed that it had disappeared. She started hitting the door with her foot, desperately wanting to flee as fast as possible. Vincent no longer existed; she was not concerned about what could happen to him next. She has one thought only in her head at that moment: to leave the place as fast as possible. For a second, she unstuffed her ears and finally touched the metal doorknob with her shaking hands, then turned the switch with all her might and opened the door wide. She jumped without looking back with her bare feet over the porch and all its steps but, her leg got stuck, and she snagged behind the last step; she fell face down onto sharp stones that covered the trail to the farmhouse. Sharp like a knife, one of the pointed stones cut in her face, and a stream of blood ran down her cheek like warm milk. The woman stood up and felt that one of her legs was stiff as the loud laughter behind her back persisted.

She stumbled her way through the dark birch alley, where her thick, dark hair suddenly got caught in one of the long birch branches, which she failed even to notice, as she continued to run down the long, dark alley towards the bright lanterns. Finally, she reached the ancient stone-wall church, knelt, and huddled up in a ball.

- God, please, protect me! I don't want to die! - she uttered, breathing heavily.

* * *

Vincent's heart started beating as furiously as lightning during a thunderstorm, as he didn't understand what was going to happen to his mom and himself. The people around him were strangers, wholly unfamiliar, and their faces didn't shine in delight or with a kind smile but, their eyes expressed heavy fatigue.

Walking through a quiet birch alley, Vincent listened as the peaceful sound of the wind spoke with him, and he tried to listen to what was being said.

- Nooooo, you should not go there! Nooooo, you should not go there! - the little guy tried to understand, whether it was the voice of the wind or whether the voice was coming from inside of his head. The loud voice seemingly was warning him of something and made Vincent tremble like a fragile aspen leaf.

Vincent pondered that, maybe, he could pull himself out of the clenched hand of the fat policeman, who was squeezing his hand so tightly. Perhaps, he could escape so he could go back to his old home and be safe.

- It's time to go to your new home! - the policeman snapped, as he nodded vigorously to a tall, skinny woman, trying to pull a smile that was not genuine, forcing the right corner of his mouth upward.

- I don't want a new home; I just want to return home to my mom, - the little boy said, sniffling quietly.

- You will live with us for a while! - the skinny woman exclaimed with a nervous smile.

A chunky blond woman approached the doorstep in rapid and pompous footsteps.

- I will show him his place! - coldly said the woman and pulled the little boy by his hand and led him through the dark hallway, past the old dresser on which stood a palm tree in a pot that was so large that it was even more significant than little Vincent. When they came closer to a white door, with the number eleven on it, the woman stopped abruptly and, with a sharp movement of her hand, pulled the metal handle down and opened the door that squeaked, as if complaining. A child's cries came from the room, as well as the sounds of kids fighting about who was going to get the best toy.

- Hello there, Valdemar, is that right? - said the woman who was sitting at the table and was pointing her hand at the other children, who were building a garage out of wooden blocks on a gray carpet.

Drops of rain were hitting at the window's panes, as if wanting to tell something, perhaps, a soul story that makes you realize you are not alone. But how can you believe them if everything you have ever known has been replaced by a dark emptiness, like a hole from which you cannot get out of?

- If only I could get out of here, then I would run away straight to my mommy and hug her as tightly as I can, - the little boy was looking outside the window, observing the dark clouds.

- You can come to play with us, - a tall boy called out from the far corner of the room but, Vincent couldn't hear him, as he was so deep in his thoughts that everything around him had become completely transparent, invisible, and non-existent. What he was feeling could only be described as a heavy concrete stone falling and plunging deeper and deeper into his heart with its splinters.

Vincent started panting more and more heavily, and his eyes were filled with a sea of tears, which turned into two great streams that ran down his crimson-red cheeks. His thoughts then got disturbed by the teacher, who ran up to him with great strides and, like a great wind, began to shake his elbow.

- I've told you countless times that you must go to eat! Are you deaf? - the woman with coal-black hair shouted, like an angry dragon, the anger of which would lead it to burn anyone who would get in the way.

These loud words cut an even bigger and deeper scar into Vincent's heart. He huddled up in a ball and then kneeled against the hard-wooden planks, which squeaked quietly under his weight. The teacher grabbed his hand and began to pull him down the slippery floor fiercely. Vincent jumped to his feet, pulled himself out of her tight grip, and ran out the door as fast as he could but, the skinny woman who reeked of sweat caught him and began to shake him hard, causing him to get dizzy and making him faint behind the small front porch, damaging his nose. Two fire flames appeared in the teacher's eyes; her yellowish teeth clenched tightly together as she muttered under her breath:

- You little piece of crap, I will show you, - she kicked the little guy with her foot, then stormed off into the room where the other kids were, - everybody in their places! - like scared little ants, the children rushed to sit down at the table like little soldiers.

- I told you not to pull the chairs on the floor!

- Sorry, miss Teacher! - the tall fellow apologized, then went quietly to the door and stuck out his head, looking at what Vincent was doing.

- Vin...can...t!!! Vin...can...t!!! Shhhh! - the boy with bushy, brown hair whispered.

- Why are you crying?

- Leave me alone! - Vincent replied, sobbing.

- Don't cry; you are not a little girl, after all! - the smiling boy said.

- You don't understand anything; get lost!

- Don't take offense! There's blood in your nostrils; here, take a napkin! The teacher slapped me once, that's why I don't like her but, you just have to obey what she says. Let's go eat together!

Vincent sat down at the table but, because he didn't want to eat anything, he hung his head and just looked down at his plaid pants. The teacher sat down in front of him, and with a spoon, she began to push potato porridge inside his mouth.

- I AM NOT HUNGRY! LEAVE ME ALONE! I WANT TO GO BACK TO MY MOM!

- Your mom is not here because she does not need you! - said the teacher and dropped the heavy metal spoon, which hit the floor with a big bang.

The minor twin brother looked at him with pity and put his hand on Vincent's shoulder:

- Don't cry! I don't have parents, too!

- We do have parents, - the other twin nudged his brother's hand and hissed, - they will take us out of here when they can.

- Silence! You all are causing me a headache! - the teacher shouted - Vincent, if you refuse to eat, then go to bed!

Vincent took off his dirty shoes and ran down to the double-decker bed, then climbed the tiny wooden stairs, and covered himself up to his head with a thick quilt, then he put his face against the pillow and tried to muffle his sobs.

- Where did you just leave your shoes? Pick them up now and put them beside your bed! - shrieked the teacher.

Vincent pretended to hear her, making the teacher even angrier. She threw his little shoes in the direction of his bed, they bounced against the wooden stairs, and the little boy winced at the sudden hollow sound.

- Oh, how I would love to get away from this place, just to be somewhere, anywhere, where it's better. No one needs me, nobody! - as he thought, Vincent stopped crying and wiped away the lake of tears from his big eyes. He imagined his mom sitting next to the bed, watching him with warm, loving eyes, singing a song about home.

* * *

Although Vincent had grown up, there were still many un-answered questions that he thought about every day. He tried to silence his thoughts, almost like turning off the television or radio. However, his views could not be silenced: they lived their own lives, prompting the same daily questions.

- What happened to my mom? - every time he asked the teacher of the orphanage where his mom was and whether she was still alive, he never got an answer.

- I have no idea! - even though the orphanage staff always said they had no clue, it seemed that they knew more than they let on and were just hiding the truth.

Vincent missed his mom a lot. He felt like his heart was con-stantly being pressed down by something like a heavy brick, and no matter how hard he tried to get it to move or drop the rock off, it never worked. It failed, even when he managed to push away his grim thoughts by running several circles around the sports stadium or listening to his favorite songs on his cherry-red player, which he had received for Christmas from American donation packages.

Sometimes he thought it would be better to leave this life behind for good. A life in which pain is burning you alive from the inside. You feel like an apple with a rotten core when you fake a smile while feeling abandoned and lonely and like you don't belong in this world.

Sometimes he thought that, maybe, his mom didn't love him. After all, she had left him in this little corner of hell, where he was a useless nuisance to everyone.

Even that one time, when mom said:

- Go away! - Vincent continued, - then I felt like a mistake pushed away, that needed to get out of the way, as fast as possible, to anywhere my feet would take me.

Is there something wrong with me? Why is everyone pushing me away? My father also had taken me away and has not visited me once, not even when I was in the hospital for several months with pneumonia. My group's teacher somehow managed to find his telephone number and even called him, his wife answered and gave the handset to him, and despite that, he promised that he would come to visit he never did.

I just don't understand; why is he like this? I could have died then, as I had late-stage pneumonia but, he didn't care; he would rather sit on his warm sofa next to his wife and sweet little daughter. I don't even know what to think, maybe he was shy about reaching out to me, or perhaps his wife forbade him to do it?

Vincent often wanted to call his father to find out what happened to mom. Why did she leave him, and did he, perhaps, know something more? The teachers, however, always made excuses, saying they would call him and then never followed through.

Vincent's diary

What are my memories of the orphanage? There are both good and bad memories; there was always someone to play with within the orphanage, many children were friendly, and each used to tell their stories about how they came here. It must be said, though, that we always sensed indifference towards us when we were small, rarely they led us out into the courtyard, and we were not allowed to sing loudly or play wars; we were immediately stopped then.

I remember a lot of kids trying to get into the nanny's lap but, she never let them and pushed them aside. The children were desperate for love but, they were pushed away, just like their parents left them away. Sometimes I think about the orphanage times, and I can never understand how parents can so quickly leave their children in the hands of fate, how they can first create and then forget about them as if they were worthless things without feelings and emotions. Don't they miss their kids? Yes, the children also ended up there for various reasons. There was also a catastrophic case of parents dying in a car accident, or one of the girls was raised by a mother who died from cancer, and none of her relatives came forward to adopt her.

In my group, two twin brothers were hyperactive and very loud. Their mom suffered from an alcohol addiction while their father was in jail for a robbery, so their custody rights had taken away. Both brothers often talked about their parents, saying they were missing mommy and waiting for her to visit them but, she never did.

I also missed my mom but, I tried not to show my feelings to the other children, and when grief came over me, I cried as quietly as I could while my face sunk into my pillow because I didn't want anyone to ask me questions. After all, then I would feel even more miserable and sadder. To be fair, I wasn't the only one who cried at nights, as many children were struggling with it, especially the newcomers, and they always asked relentlessly:

- Where are mom and dad? I want to go home!

At times like these, the nanny would pretend she couldn't hear anything, and if the child came over or tugged on her long wool skirt, she usually pushed their little arms to the side. There was indifference and rejection all around us - the two most vivid memories, there was no love, which was missing the most when you were so small, fragile, and, simultaneously, badly hurt.

I don't know why it happened so late but, my mother's relative Eva adopted me four years later. I still remember how she used to come to visit my mother when I was tiny. If you think my life has been improved, the only thing I can say for sure is that it changed a lot.

Vincent

3

Ray of hope in the twilight forest

Vincent, you're a fool! - his deep thoughts were interrupted by a guy from the backbench who punched his back hard.

- Hahaha! - A bunch of group mates laughed, and the tallest of them threw a sports shoe right at the curly-haired guy's head.

Vincent felt inner panic but at the same time unspeakable anger. He wanted to take William by the jaw and force him against the white wall but realized he wouldn't be able to do so physically

- But what if he and his friends do something worse to me, he thought and tried to count to ten to calm down a little bit.

The worst situations happened during breaks or when the teacher left the room for a coffee or relaxed from the noisy children.

The worst were Benjamin, William, and Katarina; contrary to what might be called the Holy Grail, the three villains were worthy of count Dracula's Cup. Their main sustenance was the blood of others and, to get it, they used to gather a larger crowd to pounce on the chosen victim.

Benjamin used to throw Vincent's belongings into the trash, just for fun, or to throw all the books to the ground and watch the poor guy gather them together.

Vincent turned his head over his right shoulder and watched as a bunch of guys sneered and evaluated Vincent from head to toe, watching his every move until one of them rolled his dark brown eyes and called Vincent a fish face.

One of the boys scribbled a watermelon-like face shape on a white paper, with every other tooth-colored with an ink pen, creating a wacky image.

- Look what you are! - Benjamin said and turned the page towards Vincent, with FISH FACE written in capital letters.

- Fish face! Why does he think so? Am I even somewhat similar to a fish? Are my eyes big and ugly? - Vincent thought and nervously began banging his leg against the floor.

Vincent turned red in anger and expressed his thoughts in a worried, sharp tone:

- You're suuuuuuuch an idiot!

- What did you say, fish head? You'll regret it! Do you

understand? Benjamin said with his eyes wide and, swinging his hand hard, he hit the redhead in front of him.

- Pass it on! - Benjamin threw it out as a bad joke.

Vincent felt a sharp pain in his back, and a warm teardrop flowed onto his raspberry lips. He closed his eyes and imagined that he was in a completely different place, quiet and calm, where there was the sound of the wind, the sea waves hitting the shore, and the ascent of white sand towards the sky.

- TRRRR!!! - the bell rang, and the students quickly got up from the benches and ran out of class. Vincent felt a gust of wind on his neck and face from the rapid dash out of the classroom. Lunchtime had come fast, and everyone rushed to the cafe to be first and not stand in the long lines.

- Can I sit down with you? - asked Vincent to the girls in his class, holding a red tray and smiling friendly.

- No, it's busy here! - a blond girl with clear blue eyes roared and rolled each eye in a different direction.

- Fish face! Hahahaha! - the girl sitting next to her laughed out loud.

Vincent felt the loud laughter stick like a knife into his heart, and it began to beat faster. He lowered his head and tried to disappear as quickly as possible from this unpleasant company that watched him with bare teeth.

- You can sit here! - the girl sitting alone grabbed his sleeve and, nodding, pointed out to the accessible seats.

Surprised, Vincent sat down opposite the girl and felt his cheeks blush. He took a breath to feel the pleasant smell of flowers while bowing her head and eating. He stared at her black wavy hair and lake green eyes, which shimmered like two rubies. Her lips were brightly colored with blood-red lipstick, and he noticed two small dimples on her cheeks but cute orange, tiny freckles above them. The pretty girl looked like a Gothic princess in her dark, fitted corset with sleeves made of black lace with rose patterns.

Meeting her was the first pleasant event. Vincent wanted to ask her something but, nothing came to mind, and he couldn't get even one syllable over his lips because he felt like a statue sitting opposite the charming creature.

- I wonder what her name is? Vincent thought and watched how the girl raised a glass of apple juice and rested her elbow against the table, and glancing briefly at Vincent from time to time.

The guy abruptly turned his eyes away because he didn't want to be caught staring at her.

- Who is she? What's her name? Which class she's in? I need to know everything about her! - Vincent thought and watched how she quickly drank the glass, put on her red and white checkered backpack strapped on her shoulder, and got up from the bench, and went away.

She looked a little sad and limped a little with one leg as she left.

- Why is she limping? Has anyone hurt her? - Vincent thought, and without eating, he decided to know more about this mysterious creature and started to follow her.

Many youngsters were standing at the cafeteria door and blocked the way because they were passionately talking about a football game that hadn't been fair. Still, he didn't have time to listen to this nonsense, and, above all, he had to get past the boisterous youngsters who had leaned their hands against the door hinges. Vincent purposefully broke through the group and turned his head to the right but, not seeing anything behind the many people in the long corridor, he turned sharply to the left and stretched his neck like a giraffe. Still, he did not see her and decided to run out of the long corridor to the second floor but, he didn't meet the beautiful girl there either when he ran up the steep stairs.

- I need to find her! Vincent said with his heart beating rapidly but, the bell for the next class was even more alarming.

For the first time in his life, the boy felt a real thrill, her voice, silhouette, the face was radiating a special magnetic force and loud words in his mind:

- The fateful girl.

She had everything he had been looking for and more than anything in the world; he wished he could be there for her now and could hug her hard, kiss her blood-red lips and smell her skin, and take her delicate hand, and never let go. The inner thrill was so intense that he could not calm down; he could think of nothing but the beautiful girl he met in the canteen. Yes, Vincent hated going to school, and he crossed out one day from the school diary every time he returned home with a big black cross. He used to look at the calendar and count the days when school would finally be over, and he would finally be free from all the pain, humiliation, and fear caused to him by his peers whose looks disgusted him by just looking at their smug grin-filled faces. But now, he had a reason to get up in the morning and go to that damn school with a heart filled with love, to overcome all the pain that rested on his seat like a heavy stone.

For the first time in all these years, Vincent came home in a good mood, even despite all the unpleasant events that had taken place in his class, all this became unimportant because now the most important thing was to find out who this miraculous being was who made his heartbeat so fast and thrilled all his essence.

- You could at least say hello to me! - Eva said with a frown and corrected the huge glasses on her nose, which began to slide down slowly to the tip of her nose while she continued reading the newspaper that covered her entire face.

Without answering anything, the young man ran into his room and threw a backpack onto the floor, and laid back into bed, closing his eyes; he imagined the dark-haired beauty from school lying next to him and her clear crystal green eyes staring at him.

- I could look at her forever and nonstop and be near her every single moment and drown in her presence, which is like a mysterious and inexplicable magnet, - the guy said quietly with his eyes closed.

Vincent slowly got up and sat down at his desk to start studying for the history test but, he couldn't concentrate, and his thoughts flew back to the magnetic sorceress who had charmed his heart; it seemed that Amor himself had been present and shot the longest arrow into his heart, and thus wounded him because now he feels petite and tiny in front of this being. If she wanted to, he would do anything so he could just be around her. Her proximity reminded him of the days his mother used to pick him up on his lap and kiss his forehead or say a sweet word. She somewhat resembled his missing mother - a strong but at the same time fragile woman who must be protected from the world.

Instead of repeating important chapters about the former war in world history, he pulled open the heavy wooden drawer. He took out a notebook bearing a picture of a turquoise lake on its cover, shining like a rising sun in the mirror as hope for a new beginning.

Vincent took out a black ink pen from his backpack and began to draw the Gothic princess, initially sketching the outlines of her body; he paid the most attention to her face because he wanted to draw her as he remembered her in life, to put on the wall later and look at her face when he was done. He glued his little art masterpiece to the wall above the massive desk and kissed her lips. Finally, a real moment of happiness and a desire to live, even to go to school, had entered life, just to see her again.

With his hand resting against his chin, he gazed out the window with dreamy eyes and imagined walking with her down a birch alley next to the house, leading to deep romantic thoughts.

- Ever since I've seen her, I think I've lost my mind; I've been thinking about her all the time, the unknown girl who's the most beautiful woman I've ever met. She has natural beauty, and she is also a kind-hearted, friendly person because she offered me to sit next to her and had said it in a gentle, loving voice. After all, love radiates from her like morning light in the opaquest and thickest fog.

- I want to see you again as soon as possible, - thought the red-haired guy and bit himself a little bit on the lip and closed his eyes.

- What are you doing there? Stop sleeping and start studying! Your grades are so bad, and you know that! You barely stay afloat! Don't miss your chance; you won't be anything without education! - the new mom said as she entered quickly and interrupted the dreamy thoughts in Vincent's mind.

- You better tell me how the school was today? - said Vincent's relative, scrunching her nose.

- Not too good! I don't like my classmates; they mistreat me all the time, - Vincent said and lowered his head.

- It's your fault, - she said.

- How is it my fault? She doesn't understand how I feel, and it's evident that she has never been in the same situation as me. How can she even say that? Is she the aggressor, one of them, or did she say that because she thinks I should deal with them myself but, how can I do it if there's a whole group against me? How can I handle them alone? The only good thing is that I met a beautiful girl today, and I will try to find out about her as much as possible, - he answered in his thoughts.

- Listen, I think we should go to a psychologist or psychotherapist together, - Eva said with a severe expression.

When he heard this, he felt himself boiling on the inside,

and peculiar click happened, and a surge of blood flowed in his brain, and the more he began to think about his classmates, and that he didn't have a mother next to him, the angrier he became.

- If my mom were next to Eva, she certainly would never say that - Vincent remembered that Eva always made fun of his mother Sarah because when he used to be a young child, he often heard them both arguing. At the same time, he played with his wooden bricks in his beloved corner of the room. Eva rarely visited Sarah but, when she did, she always put money on the round kitchen table with a kind of sharp gesture or resentment in her heart - remembered the boy.

Vincent approached the wardrobe, put on a tracksuit, took the bright red music player in his hands, ran down the stairs in a rhythmic step, and walked out into the courtyard. He began to run further away from home, wanted to get away from the situation, a place where he was, at least for the moment. However, he knew well that tomorrow would come again, and the old song, the old scars would be torn up again by his heartless classmates, for whom the most important thing is to destroy the lives of others to feel better themselves.

- I don't want to go to school tomorrow because I don't want to see classmates, one of those bastards threatened to do something terrible to me but, despite everything, I just want to meet that beautiful girl... God, I don't understand what I feel or want anymore but, does it even matter what I want??? I think my heart will break into a million pieces; it feels like the whole world is against me. I don't want to live anymore; every day, I force myself to get up from bed to take the first step towards pain and walk into a classroom where you're being made fun of and abject.

- I can't understand why they treat me like that? What have I done to them? It's not good at school or home - he immediately started to run through the silver birch alley with great speed and ran down the winding, rock-covered road into the dark greenish spruce forest, and continued, until one leg got caught by the root of the tree and he bruised his knee and elbow when he fell.

Tears began to fall down Vincent's cheeks because he couldn't fight everything and everyone anymore against all the unpleasant situations. He realized he was probably cursed...

- I don't want to live anymore, God, take me to yourself in your bright world! I am sure that it is much better there, and the people around are not so evil. Please, take me to my mom, I don't know if she is in your world but, since no one has answered all my questions, she's likely dead, even though all the time I still hope she's alive. Please, take me to You; I can no longer breathe this poisoned air contaminated with lies, disgusting words, contempt, and betrayal. All I ask You, put an end to my suffering! - when he said this, he turned his head towards the road and noticed that his request was answered.

He stared at the winding road, while he was standing on the top of the hill, and watched as the dark road and spruce forest became lit with sun's evening rays and was shimmering like a peculiar gem, as its elongated rays were breaking through the dark silhouettes of trees, and changed the dark colors to a lighter. He saw how the dark green color turned into pale yellow, as well under his feet; the path was glittering in gold.

The light came to him, with a breeze in his hair that created goosebumps all over his body. This kind comes when you have heard a miraculous voice singing the highest notes or listening to a melodic masterpiece by a pianist in which every touch of the key is played out with utmost love.

He felt how the sunlight broke into his heart and warmed it. Vincent felt indescribable, and that nature is talking to him in its quiet and peculiar way - there, someone loves me - and he realized it was indescribable and inexplicable.

Darkness is replaced by light; I hope my life will change if I paddle against all the storms and dark times because I can overcome any difficulties. Now I feel like I'm not entirely alone in this world, and I understand that I have to keep living and fighting; if you've fallen, you have to stand up again and again so often that you don't feel any pain anymore because it's always temporary even if it doesn't seem that way at the moment.

- Thank you for your answer, - he said quietly, staring at the light-filled spruce forest and the shiny, winding road - one day my life will be better, even if right now it's like a black pitch pit in which I'm stuck like a fly in a cobweb. I know now that I have to try to continue living and paddling through this swamps of life, - when he said this to himself, he began to smile and returned home with a very confident gait, and head held high even his bleeding elbow and knee no longer stung because it no longer mattered.

- Where were you? I am worried about you! Where did you get those bruises? - angrily said Eva and raised her thick eyebrows.

Vincent didn't say anything and inadvertently hit her hard with his bony shoulder as he passed by:

- Watch where you're going! Do you hear me?! If I wouldn't be here, you'd still be in that God-abandoned orphanage.

Vincent didn't listen to her words just kept smiling and moved towards his room.

- Are you crazy? What's going on with you? What? - loudly muttered Eva.

When Vincent opened the heavy wooden door, it squeaked hard. He walked up to the window and watched how a bulky man got into the muds and looked terrified of his dirty shoes, and shook one of his feet and wanted to shake off the sticky sand. The tall man looked towards the window and saw how Vincent looked back at him, while he didn't notice that a postal car was pulling up behind him.

The driver of the car hit the brake sharply because otherwise he would have run over the careless man and got out of the vehicle holding a giant letter:

- Look more carefully where you're going! - the driver said wryly and approached the post box of the house, which was beside the wood-carved owl, and threw the letter in it.

- What kind of letter is it? Maybe there's some news about my mom? - Vincent's heart started pounding very fast, and he rushed down the creaking wooden stairs at lightning speed.

- Where are you running again? Your knee is covered in

blood, and when are you finally going to study? You just run around all the time! - Eva was sitting on the soft couch and threw the newspaper on the table in anger.

- She should leave me alone! - said the guy and unlocked the letterbox.

- There you are! - he searched for the letter's author and was surprised when he saw that the letter was from his favorite school while tearing the letter, he became disappointed because there was a ball invitation inside it.

We invite you, Vincent C., to the Halloween Day Party!

October 31 at 18:00

Bring a basket and a good mood!

The venue is in the school's act hall.

4

The last drop of patience

A white, muddy bus arrived, and as always, it was there in the morning and waiting for its work ants to pick them up and transport them to the anthills. One of the biggest ant-hills - a crowded school full of children, surrounded by a gray, strained highway, while in its side stood a lonely, burnt-down cottage house.

The bus driver braked quickly and said:

- Time to wake up, and whether you want to or not, it's time to go to school.

- If the bus really could talk, I would reply to it. I dislike school but, I want to go for other reasons because I might meet her - the gorgeous girl with dark hair. I really can't stop thinking about her, - he thought to himself as he dreamily looked outside the window.

- Haven't you got to go to school??? - said the bus driver as he turned his head.

Vincent was frightened by the sudden question and understood that once again thoughts abstracted him, so he rushed away to get out of the bus and the unfortunate situation.

The young kids, who had gotten out before Vincent, turned their heads and giggled. With small steps, they rushed to school with the brightest smiles on their faces, as seen in advertisements.

- At least someone likes going to school! - Vincent thought to himself as he looked at the students, who were going through the asphalted road heading towards the school. Many children were intrigued by one of the students wearing shorts and a white t-shirt, so they turned their heads and discussed their thoughts about the brave boy.

- What is their business about the way he's dressed! - thought Vincent and suddenly stopped because a dancing, bright, red maple leaf flew across his face; it fell right onto his neatly polished shoe through the foggy morning in its unique way, which was the first indication that winter was coming.

Vincent reached the school door's doorknob but almost immediately let it go because he heard his phone ring.

- Hello, am I talking to Vincent?

- Yeesss...

- I apologize for calling only now. It's your father, Christopher.

- What? Vincent opened his mouth and froze like a wax figure.

- Careful! - said a girl, who ran right into his back and pushed him in anger.

Vincent walked away towards a park and sat on a white bench covered in morning dew but, he was so utterly shocked that he didn't even notice his surroundings. It felt as if it was just him and the deep voice on the other side the phone.

- Hello, hello! Can you hear me??

- Yes.

- I can barely hear you! Vincent, I hope everything is okay with you. We should finally meet to talk, and I also want to know how is your mother doing?

- Yesss, of course? My mother has been lost for many years! Maybe you know something about my mother?

- What do you mean? Don't you both live together?

- Looks like you don't know anything.

- Vincent, I want to help you in any way I can. It would be better if we met as soon as possible and I promise we will figure out something. Will you be free today after school?

- Yes, I will be.

- Let's meet at the shopping center, next to the big entrance's door, at 5 p.m.?

- Of course!

- I will be in a black leather jacket with a brown suitcase.

Vincent couldn't believe that he may hear something from his father one day. He only remembered him from a few visits but, it was all blurry because he was a small child.

- Why didn't he call me earlier? Where has he been all this time? - he felt as if the questions and thoughts had sunk him into his world, and he didn't notice that only in five minutes class lessons would begin. He rushed into his class with wide steps, and as unnoticeably as he could, he took a seat.

- You must attend class in time, you have to respect your classmates! - said the teacher and got up to open a vast world map.

- Did she seriously mean that? If only she knew how my classmates treat me, or she hadn't even noticed? I feel as if everyone is against me, even the teacher.

The rest of the classmates evilly grinned, and Benjamin said to the teacher:

- Yes, that's true! - but even just that comment wasn't enough, as Raivo tapped his fist onto Vincent's back. Vincent once again felt as the anger took over his whole body and his arms started trembling, so he turned around to the chunky boy who was sitting behind him and said:

- Stop it!

A laugh was followed from the group of classmates, and Raivo once again and again punched Vincent, as if he was desperate for the attention of others and as if he must prove that he was better and more potent than most.

Raivo took the gum out of his mouth and stuck it onto Vincent's back of the head. Vincent reached the back of his head with his hand, and at that moment, the gum fell and rolled into his lap.

- Did he just do that? I can't take this anymore! - at the moment, as Vincent said that to himself, he felt that he became a ticking bomb, filled with hatred and anger, ready to explode at the slightest movement.

As Vincent heard the sound of creaking paper, he got ready as if he came into a warzone, prepared to be attacked, and he wasn't wrong, he felt, a note being stuck on his back by a fist. Vincent didn't even turn around, he took the paper off his back and read the text aloud:

- YOU SMELL!

Vincent felt how the rush of blood started to circulate in his brain and how his mind got foggy. He suddenly jumped out from his desk's chair and hit the floor with a big bang. The teacher got so confused that she started to yell something loudly but, Vincent didn't hear that because his patience had run out. He couldn't control or stop himself anymore, so he put his arm around the boy's neck, who was sitting in the back, and dragged him to the chalkboard, and smashed his head against it. His head hit the white chalk right on today's date, and a stream of blood drained down his forehead, and thick piles of blood hit the ground.

Two of the class boys stopped Vincent, dragged him out of the class, and looked at him as if they didn't recognize him anymore. In their eyes, you could see utter shock and fear. Vincent dragged both boys out of the way and ran through the first-floor corridor to get out of the building as fast as he could. He hadn't had taken his school bag, nor his jacket but, that didn't matter anymore. The school's principal ran out of the key cabinet and yelled:

- Come back! Where do you think you are going!

Vincent didn't look back but continued to run, through the school's long corridor in direction to the birch alley, till he felt that he ran out of breath and his legs started to turn weak as made of rubber. He rested his arm on an overgrown moss linden tree and started to cry. Vincent didn't know what to do next but, all he understood was that he would not be able to return to that dammit school, so he decided to return home and get a warmer jacket and then finally meet with his father.

- I need to find out what is with my mom, no matter the cost, so that I can finally move out of here and forget this nightmare, - thought Vincent, as he wiped his tears and went into a gasoline tank store.

He placed a pack of menthol on the cashier's desk. She didn't even peek at the customer's face when she gave back the change and continued to read her yellow press magazine.

Vincent sat on a bench under the oak tree. He started coughing loudly; he felt as if he had eaten the spiciest chili pepper in the world. His head got dizzy, and everything around him got dark and spinny as if he was on a lousy carousel ride. Vincent couldn't control his legs anymore, they moved on their sides like seaweed in an uncalm river.

- I need to sit for a second, - said the boy quietly to himself.

He sat in the grass, and even though he felt utterly dizzy, he looked at the sky. Clouds danced their unique dance, and from one shape, turned into another. It reminded him of white swans swimming on a blue and smooth mirror-like river.

- That brute deserved what I did to him! Yes but, what will happen next??? Either Police or retaliation from classmates?

Maybe, I'll get thrown out of the school but, I don't want to start thinking about all of this, and what will Eva say? I hope that she won't throw me out of the house, - questions kept spinning around in his head like a windstorm.

He heard a phone ring in his pocket; worried, he pulled it out of his messy, candy paper-filled pocket. All the papers flew into the air and made an airy whirl. Vincent's heart started to beat fast when he saw Eva's name on the flashing phone screen. Fearfully and unwillingly, he put the phone to his ear.

- Have you lost your mind? I don't know what to say! Your teacher called me and told me that you hit Raivo against a chalkboard, and now, he is in a hospital, and his parents are so mad at you, and so am I! What am I supposed to do with you? What??? I might get in trouble now because of you, and you might get expelled from school, - said Eva while was loudly sobbing.

- Please, forgive me but, I really couldn't take it anymore. He made fun of me every day, and trust me, he deserved that!

- Unbelievable! Where are you now??

- I ran away from school. I'm outside.

- Get back to school, do you hear me!! And you better come home early!

- No, I've got other plans.

- What other plans? Have you gone mad?

- As always, you don't understand me! - Vincent hanged up and turned off his mobile phone so that nobody could reach him, and went home.

- Eva just didn't get me because she probably has just never been in a situation like this, when everyone's against you like a pack of wolves that want your blood. Still, this time it was different, I got the blood, and that naughty brute deserved this. He finally got this lesson because clearly his parents never gave him any borders in his entire life and always just let him do whatever he wanted to do, just like the rest of the parents of those boys. To be honest, both of his parents are complete sweethearts, always smiling and happy, and always indulge his son. Who else could ever show him his place? In truth, he's a weak fool. I've got to say that when I attacked him, he was so scared and fragile, like a rabbit or a chicken. If you think about it, what can be the worst that could happen to me? Will Eva send me to an orphanage, which either way wouldn't be worse than here, or they will expel me from the school but, if that happens, I can just go to a different school. I have very little to lose, to begin with, but the only thing that worries me is that I won't be able to see that beautiful girl from the cafeteria again.

When I am drowned in this deep swamp, I still can't stop thinking about her. Possibly my father could be my only hope to get out of this, and I have to meet him and the faster, the better - thought Vincent and unlocked the door of the house and quickly wrote a note, - *I'll be home in the evening! Vincent!*

When Vincent again looked at his wrist clock, whose glass was slightly broken by the earlier fight, only five minutes had passed. He pulled out one more menthol from his stuffed pockets, he felt like he was about to throw up, and approached the grey, sieve-type trashcan.

A raindrop fell from the grey sky that hit Vincent's pale forehead.

- Nice! - though Vincent ironically.

He didn't even blink an eye because of the sudden rain but bravely continued to sit on the white bench while was waiting for the long-awaited meeting and watched the raindrops as they hit the park's pond and made a unique, symphonic sound. The leaves of the trees were colored in red, orange, and yellow colors, they were wearing the most colorful gown dresses. The tall maples proudly reflected in the surface of the pond, and in their branches, the birds sang songs of praise and how beautiful they were, while the other leaves fell from the sky.

- I wonder, what will my father look like? Will he be similar to me? What if he is a copy of me? Is he even a good person? Maybe, I'll finally find out what happened with my mother, and if he has always known, and never told me anything, then I swear to God I'll be so angry at him!

While he was sitting in his favorite park, he looked at the old water fountain, which reminded him of an elegant, white, porcelain teacup that always works despite the cold autumn evenings and the shredded coins and the wedding locks in it. Several wedding locks and the long chains by the metal railings had connected to a small crooked park bridge, which was entirely rusty for years.

The bridge piles stretched into a shallow green pond, which was home to geese, ducks, and howling green pond frogs, which enjoyed sitting on the vast water lily leaves, the flowers of which had already bloomed.

Every time someone crossed the small bridge, a herd of duck families bravely swam closer to the people who fed them with bread. The ducks fluttered their wings and stretched their necks while dancing the waltz dance. There were also giant yellowish-brown geese in the pond overgrown with greenery. The geese showed their superiority by pecking at the ducks next to them, thus giving them the right place and showing who is the main one here.

Vincent was slightly worried that they hadn't yet flown away to warmer country because, in winter, they could not survive.

Like an invisible ghost, an older man with a beer bottle in one hand and a cigar in the other crept up from behind. The rays of his trousers were shrunken and revealed socks with red and black stripes, while his shirt was dirty with large stains. The older man's smile revealed a rare row of teeth but, at the same time encouraged that maybe everything in life is not so bad and that even in difficult moments of life, it is possible to rejoice and smile.

- May I sit here? - loudly asked the older man, as from his breath came a strong smell of alcohol.

- Yes, you can! - said Vincent as he was surprised by such a question.

The older man put out the cigar, turned to Vincent, and looked at his hair and face.

- I apologize but, could you help me out by giving me some money? - Vincent confirmed by waving his head as he took out some coins and put them in the man's hands.

- Thank you, I appreciate it, young man!

- I used to be an engineer, I must say that they paid well but, I like to drink, so they fired me; I also tried to be a taxi driver but, I went to prison for drunk driving because I caused an accident, and so no one wanted to hire me anymore. Still, I'm not upset; I don't have to pay for anything anywhere, I can watch the stars at night, and I am not a slave to anyone.

- What happened in the accident? Did you kill someone?

- No, I didn't but, the man was spending some time in the hospital to recover.

- And you don't care?

- I am not as careless as you think if only you knew! - in a gloomy tone, said the homeless man, and as if reluctant to talk anymore, he got up from the bench, dropped a cigar on the ground, and took his white bag, which was pushed against the long maple tree, and continued on his way to the stone bridge.

Vincent sensed that it was time for him to go as well to see his father now. So many events, in one day, you could make a drama series about all the events that had taken place in his life but, who knows, perhaps the future holds bright hopes, and the meeting with the father could be the solution to all the dark problems. With hopes in his eyes, Vincent quickly got up from the bench on which he had been sitting for the fifth hour and fearfully looked around him because he did not want to meet Eva, nor anyone from his school but, especially his classmates.

What have I ever done to deserve this kind of treatment? Maybe I was some tyrant in my past life, so that's why I was suffering so much all these years? I don't understand. Is this all my fault? I don't know, what could happen next??? Eve is possibly mad at me and perhaps she's searching for me everywhere.

Two young men quickly ran from the right side of the road; one of them waved his hand. Vincent's heart started beating so fast that he thought that he was about to get a panic attack. Vincent pulled the hood over his head and tried to look the other way, pretending that he hadn't had noticed the men, yet that still didn't help because the young men were rushing in fast steps towards him.

What if they are from my school, some people that know Raivo? He has a lot of acquaintances and friends, and if he wanted to, then with their help, he could take revenge on me.

- Hey, I'm talking to you!! - a tall young man was waving his hat in hand in an attempt to get Vincent's attention.

- Yes but, I don't know you! What do you need from me! - Vincent answered while rolling his eyes.

- Hello, my name is Leo, and this is Rasmus. Tell me, do you have a moment to talk?

- Tell me please, do you believe in God?

- Pff! - Vincent was relieved and understood that the usual two guys who go around the town to educate people on Religion wanted to talk to him.

- Well, yes, I believe that there is a higher power.

- What do you think happens to people after death?

- I think that people reincarnate into a new life.

- No, it's not like that! - said the tall Rasmus strictly.

How can he know that, and he can even say that with such strict confidence? Either way, I don't have the time for such discussions now! I believe in reincarnation, despite what he says, - thought Vincent.

- I want to show you this booklet! - Rasmus opened the first page.

There was a huge wooden ship in the picture that looked like a tall house at first. A grey man in the picture stood stately in the foreground, inviting him to board. His clothes resembled an ancient robe, bright purple-red, with a blue scarf hanging over his shoulders. Vincent looked more closely at the picture and noticed that the wooden ship had a large wooden footbridge on which various animals stood in pairs in a straight line, just like in the army - camels, elephants, monkeys. Still, he couldn't see the smaller animals.

- Today's people are getting closer and closer to an apocalypse.

- Do you know why this is happening? - asked Leo.

- I don't know but, my whole life is one big apocalypse! Vincent, while slightly smiling, waved his hand to them and headed downtown.

5

Are you, Christopher?

Vincent was walking through the small area of the well-known neighbourhood and approached along the muddy, overgrown forest path, which was the fastest and the most invisible way to reach the parking place of the shopping center car park. Vincent shook his head from one side to another side and looked at people hovering like a turbulent flock of birds around the trade-paved parking lots and its entrance door.

Vincent saw a tall man standing at the door of the shopping center, who was wearing a black coat and had a brown briefcase with him. He looked swamped as he constantly spoke on his cell phone and seemed to ignore the people around him. He occasionally changed his location from one place to another, and for the second time, one of the passers-by stepped on his shoe, the man disliked this situation, so he waved off his hands and turned his back, unwilling not to get any angrier than he already was.

Could it be him? - Vincent quietly determined to himself and felt his heartbeat start pounding in a fast rhythm and very loudly, so fast that he could hear his heartbeat and, likely, the whole world around him. His feet became a slight limp from the anxiety but, he cleaned up all his worries, straightened his back, and purposefully walked towards the shopping center entrance with his head up, right to the man that he saw before.

- Please look where you're going!!! - loudly determined the gray-haired man behind the wheel while slowing down his car.

- It's you who needs to! It's a car park, and I can walk where I want. You have to drive more carefully!

- This is so rude! - said the man and quickly drove into the vast puddle next to Vincent, trying to splash him but, he failed. Vincent jumped aside on a sidewalk next to the man, who was constantly on the phone.

- Would you mind being more careful? - the man growled.

- I'm so sorry! Are you Christopher?

- Do I look like one?

- I guess I confused you up with someone else.

- I guess so.

Vincent felt a little uncomfortable about the situation and also about the fact that he could've met some acquaintance from his school, so he began to fidget nervously, just like the man next to him. The man glanced at Vincent with an incredibly angry sight, so he decided to disappear on the store's first floor. Today shopping center was full of crowds of people, and it looked like they were all rushing to one of the shops, whose window had a giant poster saying discounts were available for as much as half the price. One of the women who went inside the shop with an elbow won herself space to get out of the front door before a younger couple, they frowned in dismay and looked quite shocked by such an appearance.

- I'm so sorry! - a girl dressed in black clothing passed by from the right side of the aisle. She inadvertently looked at the window of the electric device shop; her both hands were full of shopping bags.

- It's her, the beautiful girl from the canteen! - Vincent said with a smile and crept closer from behind.

Her dark hair was wet and rolled up in beautiful curls from the heavy rain, and she brushed it back slightly to her head with one hand while they bounced back in her face again. She was wearing a black coat, and black ripped jeans, with a silver chain pinned to their pockets, which was constantly moving with the girl's fast pace, while the massive headphones usually worn by DJs were wrapped around her neck.

From the gusty evening rain, her eye mascara had rained down on her two pale facial cheeks, and people who were walking towards her looked at her from head to toes. She seemed pretty sad today but, that kind of matched her gloomy gothic style and even more so brought out her deep-seated ruby-colored eyes.

The dark-haired girl walked into the electric device shop, already knowing what she wanted. She approached the music stand and looked at a black CD.

- She looks so adorable! I could stare at her all day, - thought Vincent as he walked up to the music stand and looked at the beautiful girl around the corner.

- It feels like my heart could've jumped out of my chest, - thought Vincent with a flush as he looked at the girl very slowly and with a penetrative look. The girl continued to stare at the main singer of the band HIM as if she had fallen in love with him but, when she saw the price of the CD, she put it back on the shelf very slowly, as if she was unable to decide whether or not to buy the CD or not. She left the store while was getting remarkably close to Vincent. She didn't even give him the most miniature look nor notice him as if he had never existed. Vincent heard her sad sigh and stared numbly into her face - her eyes and lips. He wanted to reach out to her but couldn't think of anything in his mind or pull even one syllable out of his lips. His lips were as if to be dried like a desert land without water so that he couldn't speak.

Vincent wanted to follow the beautiful girl in her footsteps but, then he saw one of his classmates standing at the store exit, looking at his phone as he moved towards the counter.

- At the right time, he should have shown up! - thought Vincent angrily, tightening his lip as he hid behind one of the big shelves. He noticed the familiar face of his classmate, who began to wander around the shop's window and occasionally look at the whole store as if seeking something. A giant clock was attached to the white wall, reminiscent of the timetable at the train stations, and that's why Vincent became very nervous.

- I'm already half an hour late! - exclaimed Vincent excitedly and bypassing the shop on the other side, he came out of his classmate's sight unnoticed and started running to the agreed meeting. In front of the big exit door stood a company of friends who laughed deliciously and didn't want to rush home sooner. Blocking Vincent's path, one of the women began to show the content of her shopping bag to her friend.

Vincent squealed apologetically past the chattering women and noticed an elongated silhouette of a man standing like a soldier with his hands in his pockets. At the same time, he had a briefcase under his arm, and a leather jacket draped on his back. Vincent tapped the man on the shoulder and asked:

- Are you Christopher?

The man slowly turned. He had light gray eyes and russet hair, just like Vincent's, and his face exuded a bright smile and, at the same time, a little anxiety.

Vincent drank a little bit of his water bottle, so he didn't start crying right away. Another lousy thought and he would've been in tears. The man hugged his son, and it didn't even matter that they had blocked the entrance door and that many people were strangely looking at them both because, for this short time, it seemed that the whole world had stopped and was not spinning anymore. His father's strong embrace exuded warm love and joy, although Vincent should be angry about all those years of being abandoned and living through the orphanage but, he forgave him and smiled back with a warm smile. Immediately tears began to burst through his eyes, which he tried so hard to keep to himself. Now, as they had started their path like waterfalls, he did not intend to stop crying. Vincent asked with a broken voice:

- Where have you been all this time???

- I'm sorry that it had happened but, finally, we've met now. Let's sit there in that brown roof café and talk.

- It looks like we are blocking the pathway here, - said Christopher, looking at the amazed people who stared at the two men angrily.

Vincent's father, holding his hand on his shoulder, led him in through the big door and occasionally turned his head to Vincent to see if he had finished sobbing. Vincent had lowered his head and somewhat resembled a turtle in his shell. All he saw was the recently washed floor, a few people's feet, and pair of shoes. Vincent was ashamed that someone would see him crying, so he put his elongated hood on his head. At one point, he felt that he caught a man with his shoulder, who looked at him with a furious expression as they both slowly approached a beige color cafe.

This place had a cosy sense of home. A grayish, stocky wooden bookshelf stood tall on one of the walls, and when Vincent looked at it, a tiny child approached the bookshelf and pulled one from the massive shelf. As soon as he had done so, several books fell on the light glossy laminate with a big bang, after which he began to move the bookshelf with his little hands, and the flowerpot on it moved heavily. His mother managed to run up to him and pull him off the bookshelf. She put the fallen books back on the shelf with a sharp movement. These books were utterly dusty because nobody took them out of the frame for a while, so they were standing there alone, untouched. A small cloud of dust was reflecting in the bright light of the crystal chandeliers of the picked-up books.

- This huge pot of flowers could've fallen on this kid's head, - said Christopher, grabbing Vincent by the sleeve.

- Wait a little while, and I'll put that flowerpot down, - Vincent nodded in agreement and took a seat by the window in the very corner of the café.

- He has a mom who could always protect him. I don't even know to this day where my mother is and if she's alive at all, while I've had to go through difficulties by myself because everyone else hadn't cared about me and my life, - thought Vincent and sit in one of the seats, while was watching the mother with the baby.

- I have to say we are pretty similar, - said Christopher, who came up with a coffee tray in his hands and sat down opposite Vincent.

- We're not alike because I would never leave my child to its fate, as you left me in an orphanage or when I was sick with pneumonia, - thought Vincent.

- Yes, we're a little bit similar, we have the same hair color and smile, - said Vincent as if stopping his gloomy thoughts while wiping his tears with a sleeve.

Vincent's father placed his warm hand on his arm, wanting to solace him:

- Don't you worry now, - he said in a calm, low voice.

- I want to ask you, do you know anything about my mother?

- What's happened, Vincent? Don't you live together with your mother?

- I live with my mother's sister. When I was very young, my mom didn't turn home one day, and the social service took me straight to an orphanage. Her sister Eva didn't explain anything to me and she doesn't know anything about my mom either.

- I'm so sorry about it but, unfortunately, I didn't know about your mom. She asked me not to see you anymore, and I didn't think you were in the orphanage. If I knew, I'd take you to my place.

- But why? You just accepted what my mom said. I'm your child too, and you could have fought for me, to see me despite everything. You knew that she was left alone, in need, with a small child in her arms. My mother never had any friends or relatives who could help her. She was with a broken heart. Whatever she said, she didn't mean it. Women often say what they don't think. Well, I want to know why you broke up with her!

- I'm sorry, Vincent, we met once at her workplace in a small grocery store. She was very kind, always smiling and of course incredibly beautiful. I remember she had long thick auburn hair. One day I started talking to her, asking the most verbal phrase. Do you know what time it is now? We started talking, and it looked like she liked me, so I asked if she'd like to go to the café with me? So, we met one year until you were born, she wanted us to get married but, I didn't.

- Hmmm yeah, - Vincent sighed heavily.

- Why did he do it? - Vincent couldn't understand but, he kept his question to himself.

- Were you already married when you met my mom?

Yes, I was already married at the time, we had a complicated relationship because we often argued, and it seemed she had lost interest in me, so it was that I met your mom.

- IT WAS??? Selfish! You ruined my and my mother's life! - Vincent wanted to shout out loud but, he held on and took a deep breath to calm himself down a little.

- Out of interest, tell me who are you working as?

- I'm an interior designer and architect.

- It is an exciting profession you've been chosen, then you are a little bit like an artist in your heart.

- Well, it's a pretty creative profession.

- Are you still married?

- Yes, I'm married, and I have one daughter. Her name is Laila and, of course, a son named Vincent - as if making a joke, Christopher smiled as he laughed - one day, I'll introduce you to her.

- Yes, of course, and please say where are you coming from? - Vincent replied, wanting to learn more about his father.

- I'm coming from Mars! Hahaha, just kidding, I live in the capital city. I have a lovely family, a cheerful private house, and a dog and cat. The dog is amiable, you'll like him, he loves playing but, the cat is sluggish.

Well, yes, I'm not your family, I guess, - Vincent thought to himself.

- You better tell me how your school is? Do you study well?

- I'm in ninth grade now. Exams are coming soon but, overall, my rates are reasonable.

Listen, everything you will learn in your school can be helpful to somewhere further in life. So, take this opportunity while you can because it's a unique opportunity to gain knowledge, and if you graduate with good grades, you can also go to university. What do you want to become in the future?

- I'd like to be a businessman while being my own boss.

- Being a businessman is hard work. It is important to fight for what you want in this life with your work, brain, and will. The main thing is to have a good idea and a lot of knowledge, so take that opportunity while you can and try to learn as much as possible, to have good grades and a sharp mind, - Christopher looked at his gilded wristwatch.

Vincent noticed the bright diamond-covered name of the clock logo. This is a costly watch. I guess he's doing well with his own business. Why he didn't help my mom if he's a wealthy man but, who knows? Maybe his wristwatch is just such a well-disguised fake?

- Can I stay with you overnight today? - asked Vincent to escape from the existing problems and the awkward conversation with Eva.

- Yes, of course, you can but, we have to call Eva first.

- It's okay, I'm sixteen years old, and she knows I'm seeing you today. I'm going to text her and let her know.

- Actually, I'd love to talk to her, maybe you could give me her number?

- I texted her, look! - Vincent turned his cell phone screen to Christopher that said, - *I'm not going to be at home tonight. I'm staying overnight with my father. Let's talk more about it tomorrow. Vincent!*

- Alright, let's go! - told Christopher when he stood up.

- Yes, and I have a day off tomorrow, so there's nothing to worry about because we can spend all day together tomorrow, - Vincent set his very carefree tone and turned off his cell phone so that Eva wouldn't be able to call him and make any hysteria.

Christopher politely greeted the smiling waitress and made his way through the long hallway to the dark blue tunnel leading to the mall's parking lot. A couple of cars moved slowly towards Vincent and Christopher, one of the cars slowing down and allowing them to pass through the window, so they kept going.

There weren't many cars left in the car park, as most people had already gone home as the dusk and dark evening approached. Vincent was amazed at the different contrasts of the cars that could be seen in the store's car park. There was a rusty car in the far corner, with the side rafters in purple and the front cover in salad green color, while the car next to the door looked as young and shiny as it had just been bought from the showroom. It was a black sports car, and it was so low that it could pass through any barrier, and with its speed ahead, any racing formula one car. Such a car attracted Vincent's attention but, it also caught a boy showing his thumb up and sneaking up very close to the black vehicle. Looking around in all directions, the energetic boy's mother smiled awkwardly while taking pictures of him with her rainbow-colored phone.

- Mom, take the picture so you can see the company! - the little blond boy said.

- That car belongs to him. look, he's so proud! - Vincent jokingly exclaimed, pointing out at Christopher while seeing the boy.

- That's my car!

- What, is it your car??? I guess you're some kind of celebrity then! - Vincent couldn't believe what he saw. With his mouth open, he wanted to get into it sooner because, in his whole lifetime, he had only driven a car a couple of times but, now he had the opportunity to sit with a proud smile on his face, in a modern luxury car.

Christopher pressed the car's key button, and their doors automatically opened up, looking like two large bird' wings.

- Let's go! - Christopher threw out, sitting in a soft leather seat.

The sun had already set, and large puddles were splattering loudly along the car's wing as they drove in. The vehicle resembled a mirror reflected from the car's red and white lights. The shapes of the townhouse converged and disappeared into the night's shadow of the evening. There were only a couple of shop windows, where the light was still shining, and even over a long distance, you could see the different layout of the goods. One of the showcases in various comic poses featured mannequins dressed in bright sportswear, their faces looked so natural that they couldn't tell you who was real and who wasn't if they would put a natural person next to them. As he drove onto the great stone bridge, which was illuminated in gold, there was an indescribable sight that made Vincent's heart, indeed, happy and unnoticing by him, he began to smile with his broadest smile possible.

In the distance, mountainous terrain and the winding stream stretched like an elongated snake and in a distance, there were visible several residential buildings, with golden light radiating from their windows. Vincent felt that the whole city was alive, and there was a light-filled candle in each window, which may be very small but, the light can be seen many kilometers away and painted in all its silver might. As one ray blended in with many other lights, they created a whole candlelight festival, and Vincent felt the forgotten feeling that we were all one whole, even if we differ so much from each other and often can't live with each other.

As they both left the city, the paved road became very dark and monotonous, it was surrounded only by a bushy forest of spruce and birch troughs, which appeared for a short time when the car with its bright lights lit up the treetops, their branches looked a little spooky because they resembled white, bony skeletal hands.

Vincent felt, completely tired and his legs were almost as full of lead. He sensed how his eyelids become very heavy, and he started to doze off until his eyelids closed completely slowly, and his head rested against the car's window.

- Vincent, get up. We're here! - exclaimed Christopher by lightly tapping his shoulder.

6

A visit to father

Vincent slowly opened his eyes and looked at Christopher, whose small, grey eyes reminded him of the depths of an ocean, his clothing didn't indicate that he was a wealthy man but, his smile was so pure and heart-warming.

The first thing Vincent noticed, looking out of the car's window, was a driveway illuminated by lanterns, paved in red tones, enclosed by a maze of bushes covered with lush floral patterns.

Christopher pulled a gray remote control from his shiny leather jacket and lightly pressed one of the buttons. The metal gate squeaked a little while was slowly slipping, each on its side. Vincent overlooked the vast garden; a snow-white fountain illuminated blue and purple in the middle. Still, in the middle - a figure of the Greek goddess Aphrodite held a shell in one hand and a pitcher in the other, from which a small stream of water flowed out and its tinkling sound could have been heard through the whole garden as if gently welcoming home.

Christopher quickly pulled on the accelerator pedal but, Vincent felt his belly begin to tingle, and goosebumps appeared on his hands due to the rapid speed. Everything around him was surrounded by thick darkness; all he saw was an illuminated fountain and small lamps reminiscent of miniature fairies. Arriving at the garage, which has been made of large stones, an automatic light came on, with the brightness of which revealed the veil of secrets of the late evening, unfolding in its grandeur the entire large garden and also the proud house, where the white Persian cat merged with the white facade of the building while was sitting and licking its paw right next to the small pumpkin with carved eyes and slanted mouth.

The front of the house was divided into four Greek columns, all of which were in Corinthian style, and it looked like the upper part was twirling bunches of fern leaves. Vincent started to follow Christopher, climbed the white marble staircase, which was as clean and bright as it had just been polished with wax.

He stopped to see the surroundings while his father searched for the keys to the house. Vincent noticed a round tower on the left side of the building with elongated oval wooden windows and an expansive terrace-like balcony surrounded by golden railings. The vast building was more reminiscent of a pleasing manner than a private house; at that moment, Vincent felt a little out of place here but, with an open mouth, he wondered about its luxury.

The light on one of the windows on the second floor came on, and the purple curtains suddenly moved, a blond woman's head peeking through them, tried to see why the light on the garage had come on but, as she noticed the car, she disappeared from the window altogether. Down in the gray grass stood a massive pile of orange maple leaves with a moss-colored rake on top; instead of waiting for its owner, the mischievous cat decided it would be more interesting to tap some leaves and lay down to look at the bright stars that have been seen through the ceiling of the black night's sky, only the lonely pale moon was not visible...

The bare branches of the trees were moving lightly in the autumn wind, and it seemed as if they had come to life, as their roots had drifted off the ground to walk through the fairy tale garden and was turning in a quick dance with the bright fairies and greeted the beautiful Aphrodite.

How wonderful it is here, just like in a fairy tale! - Vincent thought and watched as the tall man unlocked the large door' of the house, reminiscent of an antique cabinet, as it knocked down with a metallic click and slowly opened up and showed the finely decorated interior of the house.

At the high ceiling hung a huge crystal chandelier, shone in a wide range of colors, at one time was glowing purple tones, another moment blue on gold shades. Vincent stopped under the chandelier and turned around to get a better look at the moving colors it created; each time he looked at it from a different angle, the white marble floor was as shiny as the surface of the lake and reflected everything, even Vincent's dark blue jeans, and muddy black sports shoes that had walked through the entire city today. Vincent became uncomfortable when he saw that he had swarmed the entire hallway, leaving muddy footprints on the white marble floor.

As Christopher noticed this, he took out soft pink slippers from the shoe closet and frowned:

- Perhaps, these will fit for you? My daughter wore them but, she will certainly not object.

Vincent wore the slippers and followed Christopher down the spiral staircase and from time to time held his hand to the wooden railing, connected with wrought metal roses, which showed the finest details of the rose petals, the delicate crease of the flower, and thorns of various sizes. Various abstract paintings hung on the house's walls, reminiscent of fuzzy patches of color in multiple colors; in the farthest corner rode alone lonely abandoned reproduction of Frida Kalla, in which she was depicted as a gray deer wounded hunting arrows in the edge of the forest. Vincent came closer to see it, wanting to understand what inspired the artist to create such a masterpiece?

- She must have felt like a victim, or she's a defender of animals and nature, -Vincent wondered, not noticing how his father opened the door to a small but very elegant room.

- This will be your room for tonight. I'll let you rest since you look tired. If you want something, just say it, - Vincent's father said with a smile and left the room but, the moment when a young man opened the dark oak door he saw the cat through the narrow door gap. It ran to Vincent's feet, ready to be defended by the new guest, and stuffed his muzzle very close to his feet, then the curious cat jumped into the white velvet bed's middle, thus occupying it.

- Our hostess has arrived, this is Ronnie, she is always interested in everything! Good night, Vincent!

- Good night! Vincent replied and sank with his back on the soft bed and fell on the white kitten's tail. The graceful cat hissed loudly and proudly raised her tail, headed to the small balcony in quick steps, and jumped into a chair made of wicker while continuing to watch Vincent's every move.

Vincent wore a soft cotton shirt, which had been put on a white stool, as well as the long trousers left by Vincent's father, then he turned off the light to fall asleep but was unable to do so, perhaps because he had had a cup of black Arabic coffee with four sugars in the evening, or maybe because he had already slept a little bit on the way here, however, the Persian cat with the attitude didn't have any problems falling asleep because all day, he had been playing with the maple leaves in the fairy-tale garden. In front of Vincent's eyes, the cat closed his eyes and stretched out his stomach on the soft chair pad.

After so many years, the guy felt happy to meet his father and finally got to know him as a good person, even though he couldn't stop thinking of all the unpleasant events that had taken his life, like a black, massive, and uncontrollable hurricane. Vincent was most worried that he might be arrested for what had happened in class today or that he might even be expelled from the school. He will not finish ninth grade, and then he would never see the mysterious and beautiful girl from the cafeteria, and of course, Eva, she could abandon him and send him straight to the orphanage.

The next thing Vincent realized, he was in another place where he had never been before; he was no longer a human being but a very peculiar form - a large and heavy creature. Vincent couldn't move quickly, so he felt trapped in this new body.

The first thing he noticed was that he was at an enormous height, and his tongue automatically stretched out against a leaf of a tree he had never seen before, lifting his head over the tops of the trees, overlooking the calm sea that washed away the gray sand on its shores.

He turned his head down and noticed that he was no longer a human but, a massive creature with a long neck, even more, significant than a giraffe's neck, finally. He realized that he was a four-legged dinosaur.

His new skin was dark green moss-colored, and the body was thick and scaly. Still, when the sun shone upon him, his skin turned silvery sheen, the head seemed very small but, the neck moved like an elevator, where you could suddenly bend it, to the ground and been able to look at the smallest stone. Then you could lift it and feel like a bird in the sky, seeing the whole area and approaching the very tops of the trees. It seemed quite a pleasant feeling to Vincent. Still, he felt, in a way, trapped in his new body, unable to run fast and only be able to slowly move with his massive mass from side to side, while each step was leaving a significant imprint on the ground and was making a loud noise. Still, to make it easier to maintain balance, he had a long and thick tail that was relatively straight and more reminiscent of a paddle, and you can paddle by yourself, as you know because no instructions were given or written for you to read.

Near him, looking for something in the long tall grass, was a bull-like creature at least twenty times smaller than him, his muzzle slightly reminiscent of a bird, and each of his paws had four pointed bony claws. A little further from the lower tops of the trees, leaves were tearing by two smaller four-legged dinosaurs, who shouted as if they were communicating with each other.

The branches of the trees were moving in the distance, and from them, a gray monster's head shone, emitting loud trumpet-like screams, coming out of the overgrown clump of the forest, the gray creature twitching its big mouth, showing its sharp teeth resembling knife blades. The creature's hands were tiny but, a frightening mouth offset them. Vincent looked at the monster, which was about twice as small, so at first, it didn't bring fear but, seeing its aggressive roar, Vincent realized that he might become his lunch; it was pretty neat and moved in the direction of Vincent at high speed, its movements resembled jumping on two legs. Vincent turned his back and tried to run away with his four legs but could not move quickly because of his heavy body; the lizard-like monster had run very close, followed by another of the same creature.

Vincent realized that there was no other way than to confront his enemy, so he turned his tail directly to the lizard-like creatures in one hundred and eighty degrees. His heart began to beat fast, and as the feeling of anxiety grew, he jumped to his hind legs, lifting his torso, and jumped on top of the nearest giant lizard. The teeth of the gray creature slammed into his throat while the other animal bit into his side. Vincent fell helplessly to the ground and felt that he was no longer in control of his body, for no matter how hard he tried, he no longer could move. He could in no way avoid the bloody teeth that hit his body again and again but, miraculously he felt no pain. Suddenly, everything around blurred in a white and thick fog...

Vincent opened his eyes, and the first thing he saw was the white ceiling reminiscent of a dream he had just seen, and he sighed with relief as he realized he was alive. The plan seemed so authentic, and he still felt anxious and heard his heartbeat fast but became calmer when he took a deep breath several times. He got up from the bed and noticed that the Persian cat had been sleeping sweetly on the soft chair pad, with his stomach turned up and his head left under the tiny paw.

- What if I have been a dinosaur in a previous life? The dream seemed very real as if my brain had shown an ancient memory that had been in my mind before I was born, - Vincent thought with sparkling eyes, looking at the top of a colored maple.

He adjusted the crumpled, quilted blanket and went down the stairs to the kitchen, from which came the sound of rattling pots, and from time to time, he could hear a voice of a woman. Vincent felt his heartbeat accelerate, and his face flushed as he approached the white kitchen with a marble table in the middle, and the blond woman he had seen yesterday was sitting next to it, looking out the window at his father's car, which entered through the big gate.

As the glazed kitchen door creaked quietly, the slender lady frightened a little and came to him very close, and stretched out her hand to greet him:

- Hello, my name is Adelia. I am Christopher's wife.

Vincent shook his hand and noticed that the ring of her hand was silver-colored and with initials engraved with gold letters in the middle - C&A, next to a shining row of small diamonds, her hair was put up in a ponytail along with a hair extension pinned to it, which looked very bad as if made of synthetics. She has been painted her lips with beet-colored lipstick, and a dark liner has been wrapped around her eyes, somewhat reminiscent of an ancient Egyptian, Cleopatra. She has dressed in a white shirt depicting an owl and a black long lace skirt.

-Vincent! - The woman in front of him smiled warmly as she asked to come to sit at a table on which a breakfast omelette had already been prepared, as well as a warm teapot next to which were placed four blue cups that had been bought as souvenirs from various tropical trips. Vincent took a cup with the Alpine mountains on top and watched the beautiful landscape with his trembling hands. Christopher entered the kitchen from the hallway, wearing a red plush robe and red slippers, greeted him, looking a little nervous, and sat next to Vincent.

- I think we could spend today together. What would you like to do?

- Well, I do not know, what you would suggest?

- We could go for a walk along the sea, the ionic air is healthy! The sea is a twenty-minute drive away, very close. I often go there, sometimes alone, to sit and think about life.

- Yes, of course, I have not been to the sea in a long time.

From the side of the corridor, a young girl, dressed in a fitting sports tracksuit and holding a music player in her hands, came in with quick steps but, when she noticed the new guest in the kitchen, she stopped and was a little embarrassed, and was staring at Vincent for a few seconds and didn't know what to say.

- You're Vincent, aren't you?

- Yes, I am Vincent, and I understand that you are probably my sister. Is that so?

- It is! Yes, we have finally met. My name is Sofia

- As if not knowing whether to hug Vincent or not, the girl decided to pat him on the shoulder like an old friend.

- In which grade do you study? Vincent asked, looking at the girl's face, wanting to see the slightest resemblance to himself, noticing that her nose was as blunt and sharp as his.

- Tenth grade and you?

- I am in ninth grade now, - Vincent replied.

Vincent's mood was dampened by the idea that his mother had chosen a married man with a child, thus taking away his opportunity to talk to his father when he was a child about the things boys usually talk about - cars and boy things. He just wanted somebody who could have carried him on his shoulders while he was a child and he could have had someone to play football with but, he didn't have that, and neither he had any friends, nor someone who would give him time and even the slightest of interest. But maybe my mother didn't even know that he was married and what does his wife think about all this? Vincent thought and frowned.

- I have to go to training now. I hope to see you again, - she ran out of the house and grabbed a bottle of water.

- She will be competing soon, so she is rarely ever home, - the blond woman said while was drinking her steaming coffee in a porcelain cup.

- If you're ready, we can go now, - Christopher said, grabbing a leather jacket.

As sun rays hit Vincent's pale face, he sat in the light sand of the beach and closed his eyes, and started to listen to the still whispers of the sea, which were emitted by the calm waves, leaving behind white foam, as if they were talking in their unique way. The light blue skies almost merged with the dark blue sea, on the horizon which embraced two large white cargo ships, which had lowered their heavy anchors and stood still. Christopher took off his sports boots, rolled up both his trousers' rays, and invaded the icy water to the knees over his body with slight tremors.

Vincent came into the sea as if was looking for something. He leaned very close to the ground and put his right hand in the sand of the beach, then turned to Christopher and put a piece of green glass in his hand, which was very smooth and a bit reminiscent of an ancient gemstone.

- It looks polished enough like it could have been here for about ten years, which is for how long we haven't had met, - Christopher said hoarsely.

I always had hoped to meet you and often wondered what you would look like and whether you are like me or not, Vincent said while looking at the green shard.

- My life is like this piece of glass - neglected, no one needs it.

- Vincent, we've finally met now, and I'm sorry that I didn't find you sooner but, believe that I thought about you every single day. My son, all I want is for you to be happy and I see that something is bothering you a lot, so don't be afraid you can tell me anything, what happened.

- Hmm, where do I start, - he muttered quietly and sighed heavily - a lot has happened, lots of problems that will not leave my life and still keep driving me to despair, I do not know where my mother is, and I want to find out what happened to her. Otherwise, I feel I have to fight against the whole world alone.

- I'm sorry, Vincent but, I don't know where your mother might be? We both met for about half a year until you were born but, I already had a family, so that I couldn't be with her and when she found out that I had a family, she was devastated and wanted me to disappear from her life forever, her wish was that you and I would never meet, Christopher! - As tears fell over his cheek, Christopher said and hugged Vincent, as if asking for forgiveness, he pulled a leather wallet from his trouser's pocket and opened it, and showed a small picture of a little smiling boy with frizzy, curly hair.

- That's me! Look how stupid I look there.

- No, you look lovely there; Christopher smiled and put the small picture back in his wallet.

- I've gotten in big trouble. I've to say that I never really understood why other classmates bullied me at school and kept pushing me around every day until one time I couldn't stand it anymore, and I beat one of them.

- And what happened next?

I don't know what will happen next but, I ran away to meet you after that. Meeting you is the only good thing that has ever happened to me. Please don't leave me! Vincent began to gasp and felt two rivers of tears rain down both cheeks.

- Please don't cry but, we must return to Eva now. Please tell me, where do you live?

7

Halloween ball and surprise

Christopher pulled up to the side of the pavement and got out of the car together with Vincent, and they quickly approached the red brick house, whose backyard had been proudly marked by a stock of maple trees and the leaves painted in gold. Across the old green backyard, you could see her neighbor's gray-haired head. With sharp rapid movements, she raked the leaves that had already fallen and hummed to herself an unknown song. Christopher greeted his neighbor but, she didn't notice him because she was too immersed in her world.

Vincent felt his heart was beating faster and felt how his neck pulsated from excitement. Christopher raised his hand

and knocked on a heavy wooden door. Vincent heard the sound of slow, hollow steps approaching very close to the door. The wooden handle moved down, and its hinges squeaked with a loud noise and then slowly opened. Vincent's pale facial cheeks flushed utterly red. Eva's hand lounged through the door gap, which was on her right side of a hip. Her forehead frowned in wrinkles, and her lips squashed tightly together. Her whole face expressed the anger she felt as she boiled internally.

- Hello! - said, Christopher.

Eva, unresponsive, turned her eyes to Vincent, looking into his eyes as if trying to suck his soul out, - Where were you all night? I'm responsible for you. You can't do that!

- I met my father, - Vincent said with his hand pointing at Christopher.

Eva stretched out her hand and slapped right into Vincent's face, and with trembling arms behind one of his sleeves, she dragged him into the corridor and slammed the door shut, leaving Christopher standing with a mighty astonished expression. That awkward moment existed for a couple of minutes, and then he turned towards his car and left.

- Do you know what trouble you've made? I couldn't sleep all night without knowing where you were! My class teacher and Raivo's parents called me, the boy you attacked had been taken to the hospital! - Eva said, crying.

- I attacked! He has been attacking me all these years since I was studying here! He deserves a lesson because apparently, his parents have not been engaged in his upbringing!

- Do you even know what the outcome could be? I hope

they don't sue you! You could probably have been thrown out of school. That's what you can start thinking about! Who else needs you? Me?

- You know, if you don't like me, then I'm going to live with my father!

- To him??? Yes, I know this man is your father because I saw him with your mom long ago.

Eva began laughing out loud:

- Trust me, he doesn't need you. If he needed you, he'd never leave you. You and your mother both had nothing to eat! You both ate just bald potatoes with pure water. The fact that you are still alive at all is because of me because I was the only person who helped you both, even though I couldn't easily do it after my husband died.

- If you don't want me here anymore, say, and I'll leave you forever and will never come back! - said Vincent as if feeling remorse. He tightened his lip and bowed his head.

- Well, where are you going? Where are you going? - Eva was yelling loudly, waving with both hands.

- I'm leaving with my father, and I will move to another school where there will be more normal peers and will get rid of the most insane problems, I've experienced in all this hell!

- Well, if you want, you should finish ninth grade at least. First, finish it and then do as you know! - Eva said.

Vincent's diary

Hey, my dear diary! I decided to tell you how I've been doing lately. I have to say that my life is not dull because events follow me one after another. The first day at school after the accident with Raivo was terrifying because I didn't know what would happen to me next. It seemed that all his friends wanted to stumble upon me, and I didn't know if I would return home at all. When I returned to school, I felt like I was in the field of war and looked in all directions, waiting from which side to start a fight or getaway.

I entered the classroom a little late because I didn't want to meet my classmates while they were all in the hallway, in one big crowd. My classmates looked at me in silence with a sharp eye but, the teacher looked angriest and sent me straight to the school principal for discussion. I told her everything and that I had constantly been ridiculed in the classroom and could no longer stand everything happening to me. Miraculously she didn't shout at me, only determined that I shouldn't do it again in the future. I don't know if it was a warning or if she was too engrossed in her work, sitting at the large pile of papers, her whole table covered with various folders and documents.

You're going to ask, what happened to Raivo? He had a mild concussion, and he wasn't at school for a month. His parents were angry and came to talk to Eva and me at home. Eva kept apologizing and started crying. She told me to apologize but, I made no apologies. I told myself I was tired of him regularly getting me around in class. Raivo's parents left angrily, the woman was still shaking and saying something to herself but, I didn't care even if she was too hurt. I also was all these years...

I have to say that the children around me at school finished making fun of me because it looked like they were afraid of me.

Sometimes there were ugly remarks but, all the mockery went away, and if there was sometimes something, I was just ignoring it. You could say that I was at school, like invisible glass, which supposedly was but, no one paid attention to me, and I didn't mind it because it was much better than when you have been physically beaten or when you're being mocked every day.

Once, in the school hallway from the parallel classroom, a student with whom we had sports classes together called me a murderer, just at the exact moment when the beautiful Gothic girl from the canteen passed me by, and then he started laughing at how she had been dressed. I was shaking with all my anger internally just like a gun with munition, ready for the trigger to be moved but, not because they were laughing at me but, because they humiliated and laughed at the girl, in which eyes I saw the only true meaning of everything. She was the only reason I went with a smile on my face to school every day, and when she passed me by, I was altogether nervous and thought that my heart would jump out of my chest. She was the only reason I decided to go to the Halloween party. Eva was so happy because she thought I was trying to get involved in school and make friends with classmates but, that was not my goal.

And finally, in my life, something happened, something I wanted; I managed to dance with my love. I found out that her name was Maggie, she certainly didn't know who I was because I was wearing at the party a skeletal outfit. My face was completely covered with a skull mask but, she had dressed up as a witch, and although there were a whole bunch of friends around her, she did agree with a smile on her lips to dance with me. Maggie tried to find out my name in every way and which class I had been studying in but, I kept lying to her and said that my name was Victor and I was from eleventh grade. I said that because I knew girls liked older guys, and she seemed interested in me. I was the happiest person in the world that night, and it seemed that all the bad things that had happened to me were worth it because of this one moment and as long as I had the hope of meeting such a miraculously beautiful goddess as Maggie.

In her charming eyes, which featured her whole beautiful soul, I would be able to look forever and get intoxicated like from the most robust wine. For now, that's it, and I'll see you soon!

Vincent

The evening slowly began to twilight, and behind the windowpanes, the wind was quietly rustling, moving its smooth branches and rusty leaves. A tear-off calendar has been pinned to the reddish wallpapered wall with a needle, with a day October 31 on top of it, while a school's invitation to a Halloween party had stuck next to the calendar with duct tape on the wall. When Vincent walked to the wardrobe door, he crossed his arms and smiled as he looked in the bright mirror.

- Today is the day! - he thought and opened the closet door; one of the hangers hung the Halloween ball gown he had bought the day before, which he found at a local autumn market from a cheerful woman who kept laughing as if she had drunk something more substantial. He stretched his hands towards the Halloween outfit and gently ran over it. The most impressive part of the outfit - a mask that looked like a real skull, forcing red blood to pour from his skull against red vesicles. Vincent grabbed a long black robe so long that he even covered his burgundy-colored lacquered shoes.

- Hopefully, I won't stumble behind this long rag, - thought Vincent, put a skull mask on his face and the elongated hood over his head - just one more thing to make me look perfect, - thought Vincent, and pulled out a plastic scythe from underneath the closet.

Eva entered Vincent's room and rolled her eyes out of surprise, then moved closer and looked at the skull mask as if she had never seen anything like that in her life. The relative's facial expressions changed like the colorful chameleon and drove Vincent a mighty fit of laughter. Vincent couldn't stop his fit of hysterical laughter and began pounding with a plastic scythe against the grayish wooden floor at a ferocious speed.

He leaned closer to Eva's left ear and whispered:

- I'm Death!

Eva called out loud in a terrified cry:

- Don't come to me like that! I don't like it!

Vincent moved a scythe of his costume with rapid strokes, which was more significant than himself, and moved behind Eva.

- Hey, get away from me! You should be back home on time, not like the last time you got in trouble and didn't stay at home overnight. This time you better be home on time! Did you hear me? - Eva loudly determined and left Vincent's room, slamming the door behind her with a big thud.

Vincent put his cell phone into his trouser pocket, which had already been stuffed with a coin-filled wallet, so he walked down the stairs, holding the long robe with one hand. He opened the blue-painted door of the house with a sharp swing of his hand.

He took a deep breath and inhaled the air of autumn, feeling its refreshing scent and touch of wind, gliding the long robe as if the wind itself was welcoming. Tiny droplets of rain fell on Vincent's shoulder, reassuring and saying that everything would be fine and don't worry!

Three little girls dressed in various quirky outfits and held small empty baskets and were rolling in small steps over the stone-battered road in a small stride. One of them looked closely at both sides of the road, occasionally looking at one side of the road and then on the other side. She was wearing a white sheet, and just to see something, the girl had cut two holes in the eye areas. Every time she turned, she held a fluttering sheet with one hand and the other hand on to her friend, who was dressed up in a round pumpkin costume. The girl, dressed up as a pumpkin, didn't notice a bus speeding as she crossed the road, that immediately was about to hit her in full readiness because the driver, at that point, had turned his head in a completely different direction, and didn't notice the creatures of short stature in the dark twilight. Vincent was running towards the bus as fast as he could and waved his scythe but, it only distracted the driver, and he stared in amazement at Vincent, who reminded him of a manic hero of a horror movie. The driver nervously ripped his hands off and became a little irritated, so he pressed the accelerator pedal till the end, just a few centimeters away from the little girl, who couldn't see the approaching giant bus behind her puffy costume. At the last minute, a girl dressed as a mouse pulled her friend behind an orange jacket hoodie, and Vincent sighed in relief.

- Look on the road! - The girl in a mouse costume screamed at the pumpkin.

- Look across the road! - One of the girls exclaimed and pointed the finger at Vincent, who was standing under the bright lantern on the opposite side of the road, whose light occasionally twitched. At his feet, the wind had brought maple leaves and twisted them into a tiny whirlwind of tornadoes, making the image of Death very alive in the eyes of the little girls.

- AAAAAAA. Let's get out of here! You see, there's Death. He wants to kill us! - said the girl with the big mouse ears. She ran ahead of her friends without even looking back, and a couple of candies in her basket fell out onto the paved sidewalk.

- Wait for me! - Slowly, behind her was walking the tip-tipped pumpkin. Because of her awkward costume, she couldn't run fast and unsuccessfully stumbled behind one of the squashed cobblestones. Vincent wanted to help the girl to get up, so he ran to her, she tried to get up with a great effort but, there was no way to do that because when she shuffled, she fell back again and again from side to side, in the same usual place, next to the large pool of rain.

Vincent set aside the scything, and leaned close to her and stretched out his hand towards her, and said:

- At least you didn't fall into the puddle!

The girl began to scream in great fright as much as she could, attracting the attention of the people around her, until one gray-haired lady opened the window and looked both ways.

- Leave the girl alone! Did you throw him to the ground? - she asked angrily.

Vincent didn't even try to answer, just looked at her side and frowned in anger, then grabbed her by the elbow and tried to push her away from the road. Her entire back was dirty with gray sand, and, as she stood firmly on her feet, she turned sharply to the other side to flee at as high a speed as her legs could bear the heavy pumpkin costume and forgot her empty basket of sweets in a large puddle.

- Hey, you forgot the basket! - Vincent raised the wicker basket high in the air and loudly exclaimed.

- Stop making noises around here! - Against the window-sill, the lady which rested on her elbow exclaimed.

- Yes, I think I have been scaring everyone in this costume and even have been invoking life-threatening situations with my presence, - Vincent said quietly to himself and looked nervously at his wristwatch, - I still have plenty of time.

The streets were empty tonight. Vincent's shoe's soles hit the paved road, and their clattering sound echoed throughout the linden alley. As he approached the school along the winding dirt road, chattering voices could be heard in the distance, louder than each other. At the school's big door' stood a bunch of young people dressed up as each other brighter. Most of them were posing for an elderly photographer showing quite a variety of freak antics that drew laughter to the people around them rather than the horror moods of the film from which they had drawn ideas for their masks and costumes. Vincent spotted on a small bench a couple of his classmates, all dressed as vampires, they all had bright red lipsticks, and their eyes were painted with a fuzzy black pencil, with their looks, they could be spotted even from the edge of the moon. The girls were so excited about their appearance that they couldn't split the little mirror. They occasionally looked into the mirror and pulled it out of each other's hands from time to time.

- How many problems because of one little mirror, - Vincent thought and tried to hide behind the tall mummy, who was lurching from side to side, swarming into his image. Vincent, more than anything, didn't want to be exposed to his vision of Death so that his classmates would notice him in any way.

A guy walked over and tapped him on the shoulder from behind:

- Are you, Nelson?

- No, I am not! - Vincent replied and looked as the guy approached several people while searching for his friend. Several people from the front noticed Vincent's skeletal costume and began to compliment him, and at times joked how good he looked and asked not to harm them.

All this brought even more to the attention of those around him, and the whole bunch of students standing at the front at the big school's doors, including vampires, turned to Vincent's side and looked at his ghostly costume in admiration.

- I wonder who he is? - One of the vampires asked her friend.

- I hope they will not start talking to me, - Vincent said quietly to himself and rested with his back to the wall and tried to be as small and invisible as possible. Vincent passed by Benjamin with his two other friends who seemed to be tipsy and moved closer to vampires; when Benjamin slowly crept in the crowd, he noticed Vincent's outfit and rested with his elbow against his shoulder:

- That's impressive!

Vincent pushed his hand aside and felt that his heart began to beat faster, and tact of anger hit his chest. Benjamin dressed up in a striped prisoner costume and found himself very iniquitous while standing next to vampires who laughed at his coordination problems.

While Vincent was crossing the entrance door, a weird-looking zombie greeted him and handed out green neon-colored entrance bracelets to all the guests. He gave everyone a kind smile that looked rather comical from the sidelines because he saw a smiling zombie. There was a thunderous sound of drum music from the school's act hall but, the music had been a little bit stifling by chattering conversations of partygoers.

Carved pumpkins sat on the windowsills of the school's room, and colorful maple leaves had glued to the window-panes. Vincent noticed that unfamiliar faces also gathered for the event. He saw young people who stood away from the other students in their groups and chatted cheerfully. Vincent walked to the School's great hall, and climbed the white stairs, and noticed that some younger girls in the classes were standing with their backs and were leaning against the white window sills, and from time to time giggled at the sight of a Ken-like guy dressed up as Zeus who had covered his bottom with a blue silk sheet but, left his top completely nude as if boasting about his athletic physique. One of the girls smiled flirtatiously, ran up to the muscular guy from behind, and tried to pull his undercoat but, it didn't work out because it had filled with a tight rope-like strap. The Ken look-alike turned sharply and gave the girl a destructive eye but said nothing and went into the ballroom from which, through the doors, could clearly notice colorful rays of disco lights that were watering in all colors and were jumping along to the melodic rhythm of the music. Vincent followed the Greek God and hung his head while was laughing at the women's wig he was wearing on his head and occasionally hung it in the right place so that it wouldn't fall to the ground.

The first thing noticed when Vincent entered through the hall doors was the thick smoke that covered the entire ball floor. The whole hall was crowded with people, and at first glance, it was difficult to notice even what was happening on stage, so he reached out to toe and saw that a DJ's table had been installed on the scene. A pirate-like guy was moving vigorously at the rhythms of music and had tied a red scarf around his forehead and occasionally raised his plastic sword in the air

- I'm sorry! - A witch with a pointy hat reached up to the doorway and a little bit poked Vincent's hand.

She tried desperately to get by the thick crowd of people as she noticed her friends were waving with her hands and were showing her to the free space at the table she could sit down at. One of the girls even stood up and tried to squeeze through the group in front of them. She was from another school and seemed like they didn't know what to do next, as they looked around in wonder.

Vincent looked at the girl who turned her head in his direction, and he suddenly froze like a block of ice because he recognized her, she was the same girl Vincent so often dreamed about and couldn't throw out of his mind, the girl who had wholly charmed him.

She's chosen to be a witch, as much as she had stolen my bewitched heart, - Vincent thought and squealed through the thick bunch of people closer to the pointy hat.

The girl sat next to her friends in the very corner of the room and got excited about the Halloween party decorations set in the middle of the table. Maggie took a small carved pumpkin in her arms and kissed it, and left a red lipstick print on its cheek.

- Oh, you are my little pumpkin! - While laughing said Maggie and looked at the disco ball shining in the ceiling and, for a moment, she seemed like she remembered something and became a little sad.

Vincent sat down at the nearby table, right next to mummy he had previously noticed at the school's entrance door. Several people around him asked his name but, Vincent didn't hear because he was too focused because he was looking at Maggie's every movement and was listening and trying to listen to what she was talking to her friends.

Maggie sat near the handsome Zeus, who looked hungry for the girls' attention, put his hand on her shoulder, and occasionally whispered something quietly into her ear. Maggie's best friends were holding hands together with some other girl, and they jumped on the stage and left the witch alone with the flirtatious new boyfriend. Vincent felt that his cheerful mood quickly disappeared, as gray clouds of rain before a thunderstorm and flashes of lightning appeared in his eyes. He became very nervous and felt like he had already lost all the excitement, his head was hurting again, and his hands were shaking.

- You look good! Is there a desire to know me? - Zeus asked while was putting the green wand on the windowsill.

- My name is Maggie, a dark-haired woman said with a smile.

- I'm not from this school but, I used to study here for one year but, I switched to another school because I changed my place of stay. Sometimes I miss my buddies but, I can survive it. Tell me something about yourself!

- What do you want to know? - as her lips touched the earlobe, the girl said.

- Ah, you are a hot girl! - the guy smiled and put his hand on her knee. The girl winked at the divine image with one eye and added a blood-red drink to her lips, which swayed from the rapid movement, and spilled right on top of the young man's possessions.

I'm sorry, it was an accident, - Maggie said while laughing loudly and trying to wipe the dark stain with napkins.

- That's okay, I'm going to the bathroom, please just don't go anywhere, my beautiful girl!

Vincent looked at the guest, sitting right in front of him. He recognized him because he had seen him before; the young man showed great interest in his unusual costume, so he leaned across the table and looked at his mask by head tightening, very close to him. Vincent squeezed a red bladder into his hands, and a thick, blood-like liquid flowed out of his face; and on the other hand, he pulled into a fist and tapped the table so hard that all the dishes liquefied with a mighty bang. Maggie was sitting near Vincent, and when she heard the noise, she turned her head towards his side.

The man opposite began to waggle his head like a rapper:

- Yes, that is an actual outfit! Where did you buy that outfit?

- I had it in my closet ages ago! - Vincent said.

- My name is Nicholas! I came here because my brother invited me to this party. Look, that mummy, it's my older brother!

- Today, there are two mummies. Oh yes, Nicholas, now I remember where I had seen him, we used to go to kindergarten together, and we used to be best friends, and from him, I learned that other families have fathers, not just moms. I'd love to ask him many questions but, I don't want him to know who I am! Since childhood, his mom had known my mom, and they were good friends. Maybe he knows something about my mom? - Vincent thought and looked outside the window while was watching how the disco lights broke out into the schoolyard and illuminated the tops of the spruce trees in purple and reddish tones. He didn't see anything more because pitch-black darkness had set in; only the stars shone brightly in the sky and somewhat resembled the sun hares formed by the disco ball that bounced restlessly on the dark walls of the hall.

While Vincent looked outside, he didn't notice how Maggie's friend got to the table and started to talk about the half-naked guy.

- Did you see his muscles and stomach press? Said the girl sitting next to Maggie and pretending like she was fainting and put her head on her shoulder.

- So handsome, you must take him! We specifically left you alone with him! Tell me, where did he go?

- I inadvertently poured out grape juice on him. I don't know how to say it, - Maggie whispered and stretched out a very long neck while was looking around.

- Well, where is he? Did he go home? - intrigued asked one of the girls in a cat's costume.

- He went to the bathroom but, who knows, maybe he went home. I hope he didn't go home because I already miss him, - Maggie replied and grabbed her friend's hand.

- Nice to hear that you miss me! Will you come to dance with me? - smiling from the corner, Greek God emerged and took her hand.

- He's back again! What does he need from her! - Vincent determined in anger and noticed that he had said his thoughts out loud and drew the attention of mummy, who began to sneer loudly, trying not to laugh but, relentless laughter came through his lips.

- Yes, of course, I was already very bored while waiting for you, - replied Maggie and winked with one eye and hung her hat to one side, slowly getting up from the soft chair.

- She's drunk! - Vincent said aloud.

- Oh, you mean the girl who's dressed up as a witch! - the chubby mummy asked and stared at Vincent with his eyebrows tightened.

- Yes, it's the same. I don't understand why she even agreed to dance with such a jerk, - Vincent said annoyedly and watched with irreverent eyes as they both hugged tightly, and Maggie put her head on his bare shoulder.

If you like her, take the opportunity, and invite her to one dance during the evening, - suggested the mummy sitting next to him and fit his loose pieces of gauze from time to time.

- Yes, invite her to dance, what can you lose! - Nicholas reached out his glass towards Vincent's, wanting to chime it.

- He's right; what can I lose? - Vincent thought and stood up with the army's readiness to go against the bulky Zeus.

- Death and Zeus, - that's going to be a mighty duel, - said the quiet Baron, who hasn't said a word because he was too busy eating.

- These chocolate cupcakes are so delicious. My mom never cooks them for me! - the Baron said with a full mouth.

Vincent burst right out in the middle of his classmates while watching Maggie and the athletic guy enthusiastically, dancing tightly at the lyrical music. Vincent walked very near the dancing couple but, they were so busy with each other's presence that it seemed that no one in the world existed, just the two of them. Right under the disco ball, they slowly swirled from side to side like figure skaters. A couple and a tall, lean man approached and touched Zeus' back as if trying to get attention but, he pretended not to notice them.

Just two steps away, Vincent stopped, and his heart started beating faster because he noticed Maggie's smiling face and glowing green eyes, while her dark bushy hair moved with every movement she made. He stood right in front of her and imagined he was the guy who had been hugging her body very tightly and was now spinning her in a swirling dance. As the music tact stopped, the slow song was replaced by a fast and rhythmic song, and he heard some words of which were sung along by a bunch of friends next door, which had gathered in a vast circle. One of the men inadvertently bumped into Vincent and unrepeatably continued his energetic dancing while was walking diagonally through the entire hall.

Vincent caught Zeus staring at Vincent, seeming to be the first that noticed his frozen standing among the dancing Halloween guests. Quite unexpectedly, Zeus let go of Maggie's hands and kissed her on her delicate cherry-colored lips as she touched her neck. Maggie closed her eyelids and flapped her long blue lashes. Zeus's touches became braver, and he drove his palms across her entire back.

Vincent's heart was in sharp pain like a pierced iron arrow, and his many issues were replaced with complete emptiness and weakness. The sad mood engulfed his whole body like poison. He no longer wanted to fight, even for one of the warm smiles that she could give him because he knew that he would never be as charming and handsome as this hypnotic Zeus, who had charmed most women at this ball because from time to time beauties with glowing eyes looked at his whole body as some kind of tempting cake, which, if they could, would be swallowed in an instant moment without even blinking eyelids.

Vincent felt devastated, and his heart shattered into tiny fragments; a tear went down his cheeks and fell into his open lips; he turned towards the door and was already taking a step to leave this place when someone pushed him aside. Vincent's classmates passed by at high speed, right in the direction of a sweet couple. The blonde girl took the teeth of a spicy vampire out of her mouth and began whacking the long-haired boy with her skinny fists, who was engrossed in the sweet kiss trap; it looked like he awoke from sleep when Zeus recognized the vampire girl with bright blue hair.

- It's Wendy! My classmate! - Vincent thought when he noticed her face.

Wendy pushed aside the confused girl and hit a slap right into Zeus's face with all her might. The hit was so loud that everyone dancing around them stopped like frozen poles and watched the enraged vampire.

- How could you do that? Do I mean nothing to you? You're

a villain! I hate you! - The angered face was replaced by despair, and she tried to hide her tearful eyes behind her palms.

- What are you doing here? I thought you said you were going to the countryside this holiday? - the guy asked.

- Are you stupid? Is that's the only thing you can tell me?

- Please forgive me. I don't know what happened.

- It's over between us! The girl, yelling loudly and left the ball while pushing aside everyone who happened to be on her way.

- That's what you need, Wendy, that's what you deserved! - Vincent said quietly to himself.

- Why do you keep staring at me all the time? - As Zeus passed by Vincent, he called angrily and tried to catch Wendy, who was running behind her, and left Maggie alone in the middle of the hall as if she didn't even exist.

- I think the party is going to be a whole loaf! The school DJs pirate occasionally raised his plastic sword and turned the music even louder, so his lungs were weltering with the big tumbling rumbling.

Maggie's face showed deep sadness, and she lowered her head and returned to her table, not noticing that she was running into Vincent.

- I'm so sorry, can I go, please?

- Beautiful witch, don't be sad, please, it's not worth it, you should better smile and tell me, - Vincent exclaimed loudly and stretched out his hand, - will you come to dance with me?

She smiled and put her hand in his.

- Your eye mascara is a little smeared, - Vincent touched

her reddish facial cheeks with his fingertips and stared at her soft lips, which looked as sweet as ripe peaches.

Vincent couldn't take his eyes away from Maggie's crystal-clear eyes, which were as green and deep as dangerous swamps, in which once trapped, you could never get out again. While Vincent was staring into her eyes, he felt that there was a whole world in her eyes, and her lips, like a hypnotic pendulum, drew all his attention, and he couldn't look at anything else than her lips, more than anything in the world, he wanted to kiss them. From time to time, she occasionally fitted her dark wavy hairs with fingertips passing through them, and her eyes looked directly into Vincent's glowing eyes.

- Who are you? - the girl asked curiously, looking at Vincent's skull mask.

- If you give me your phone number, you'll find out.

- I don't know you to give you my phone number.

- You know me because we've met at school before.

- Where exactly? What's your name and in which class are you?

- You'll find out someday but, not today!

- Well, please tell me, - Maggie said with a melancholy smile and tried to pull off Vincent's mask with both hands but, he grabbed both of her wrists and took them off.

- Okay, if you don't want to say who you are, then I don't know with whom I'm dancing, and maybe we should stop now because we already danced two dances.

- Why? Do you want to leave?

- I'm not in the mood, I'm sorry.

- Wait, my name is Victor, and I'm from the eleventh grade! Listen, you shouldn't be so sad because of that guy with whom you had danced tonight. You could find someone who would appreciate you more, and that one maybe can be me, - said Vincent while was staring into her eyes, frozen, and was holding her hand. She didn't answer anything and pulled her hand and slithered it out of Vincent's rooted fingers and headed towards the door exit.

Vincent returned to the massive wooden table covered in orange tablecloths and sat down in his favorite seat just outside the window in a place he had sat at most of his time.

- You did it! - Stretching towards the palm and with a kind smile on his face, said a childhood friend, Nicholas.

- What did he do? - the stocky Baron asked and laid down in his chair.

- He invited a girl he likes for a dance. Just look, how he stares at her, - the mummy said.

- Which one, you mean the girl dressed up as a witch?

- Yes, the same, Mr. Earl!

- Oh, she? She is my classmate, - taking a handful of chips into his mouth, said the Baron in the sand-colored suit.

- If you want to, I can give you her phone number. Look, I have a class magazine with me, - Baron pulled out a black backpack from underneath the table and put the green-lidded magazine on the table with a severe facial expression.

- Why do you have it? Vincent asked.

- My mom's a teacher, she gave me to take it home but, I haven't been home yet, so you're lucky.

As he crossed his finger across the list of the students, Baron stopped by Maggie's name.

- Look at her grades in math, eight, nine, seven, and even ten, - turning the back pages of the magazine, the chubby guy nudged Vincent with his elbow, - and look, there is her phone number.

Vincent pulled his cell phone out of his pocket, clicked on the unlock button on the screen, and noticed that it was completely discharged.

- Does anyone have a pen? - asked Vincent to his new friends at the table, who he had met during the evening.

- I don't have, I'm sorry.

- I don't have either, sorry, friend.

Vincent couldn't miss an opportunity to find out Maggie's phone number, so he ripped out a page of the classroom's magazine with student addresses and numbers and was gazing at her name between the lines as obsessed.

- Are you crazy? My mom will tear my head off! Give me that page back!

- Forget it! - Vincent stuffed the magazine's page into his pocket and left the ball, and glanced over her shoulder one last time at Maggie, who was talking to a blond girl at the windowsill and occasionally whispered something in her ear and didn't pay the slightest attention to Vincent.

8

An angel in a dream

Even though the surface of the small river had frozen, it continued to flow its way quietly, and it seemed as if it spoke only a language known to itself. Vincent sat down on the old, stout stump and watched as one of the snowflakes was swirling and fell into his palm and didn't melt at all. Snowflakes began to fall like beans, and in a short time, the withered grass was covered with a thick layer of snow reminiscent of a bride's veil. He pulled his legs out of the thick blanket of snow because he felt how they became cold, and light tremors crossed his body.

Vincent climbed onto the withered stump and looked at a place where the river branched into two equal parts which were gleaming like gold. He decided that he wanted to take a closer look and in a short moment, he started to run towards it. He felt surprised that the place hadn't frozen and marvelled at its golden glow from the sun in the sky. The long seaweeds were moving smoothly in the water and, from time to time, sounded like a delicate melody. In the middle of the river were gracefully standing many white-water lilies like a divine work of art. They were so many that you could sit by the shore from morning till evening and still couldn't count all of them. The petals of the water roses had opened, and black butterflies sat on top of some of them; when they had noticed how Vincent was slowly approaching, they flew into the blue sky and the white flowers slowly closed. Vincent came closer to the river and dipped his hands in the water and wanted to grab a piece of green glass that looked the same as had given by Vincent's father, which he had found washed ashore.Even though the surface of the small river had frozen, it continued to flow its way quietly, and it seemed as if it spoke only a language known to itself. Vincent sat down on the old, stout stump and watched as one of the snowflakes was swirling and fell into his palm and didn't melt at all. Snowflakes began to fall like beans, and in a short time, the withered grass was covered with a thick layer of snow reminiscent of a bride's veil. He pulled his legs out of the thick blanket of snow because he felt how they became cold, and light tremors crossed his body.

- You can only find such, in the sea, - Vincent thought when he heard the sound of waves behind the long reeds. He jumped sharply on the other side of the river, at first, he jumped on a huge rock and then jumped on a very flat rock until he had finally reached the other shore. He slipped through the long stalks of grass that went over his head, finally reaching the coast of the river.

He couldn't believe his eyes because he noticed that in the middle of the river's clear water was swimming, a female radiating a golden glow around her and illuminating the dark river like a bright lighthouse. She admired the little water waves as she splashed them with her hands and was laughing that reminded the sound of symphonic bells. She overlaid her long charcoal black hair over her shoulders and proudly stretched out her white, swan-like wings while was splashing tiny drops of water that, in golden light, resembled like shiny pearls. Vincent wanted to come closer at the miraculous being, so he stepped into the ice-cold water as quietly as possible. Still, the divine being heard him, so she turned quickly in Vincent's direction while was covering her bare breasts. Vincent's heart began to beat so fast that it seemed as if it would break through his body and fall right at his feet. Her face was so familiar and beautiful; only her ears looked different because their upper part was sharp, just like fairies.

- Maggie? Are you there? Unable to hold himself in the reins any longer, Vincent ran to the beautiful woman who was able to quench his hunger for true love, which raged in his heart like a foolish storm.

He plucked the water rose near him and put it in the beautiful creature's wavy hair and hugged her wings very tightly because he didn't want her to let go ever so she wouldn't fly away, and kissed her on her soft raspberry-colored lips.

- I love you with all my heart. Just don't leave me, don't leave me alone! - Vincent said while was stroking his head and pulled his fingertips through her golden, light illuminated hair.

The first rays of the sun had come with breeze wings and were breaking through the windows panes and gently stroked Vincent's face and woke him up from the deep sleep. Vincent saw that his legs were not covered with a blanket and therefore had become very cold, just like in the dream he had just seen. Still, Vincent could be ready to endure the ice biting in his feet forever, as long as, he could be next to the golden mystical creature with angel wings.

Vincent sat down on the edge of the bed and rubbed the sleep-out that had thoroughly clenched his eyes. Like a cheetah, he ran to his Halloween costume and put his hand in the pocket of his black robe, and touched the crumpled sheet of paper with beautiful handwriting in which was written The girl's phone number and home address. His hands trembled with inner excitement and happiness; he felt how his fingers automatically pulled a white paper and a blue ink pen out of the desk drawer and began to write a thought held in his heart, which had finally broken out of his mind shackles and was waiting to be handed over to the special girl.

* * *

Hi, Maggie!

Thank you for the dance you gave me at the ball, you made me the happiest person in the world because of this short moment

I finally was so close to you and could look into your beautiful, magical eyes. Since I first saw you, I have to say that I couldn't stop thinking about you. You have truly natural beauty, and you are the most beautiful girl I have ever met.

I used to look for you between school breaks and walk down all the possible corridors just to see your gorgeous face and beautiful green eyes, and even sometimes after school, I walked around the city while was hoping to see you. In those happy short moments, when I saw you at the school, I felt in my heart that you are the main reason, why I could force myself to get up in the mornings and go to school, where I had felt very lonely. Still, I think you might have felt the same way because I watched you at school and noticed that you often walk to school alone.

Maggie, if you feel the same way, give me one hint, and we could both be together and end this torment.

I don't know but, maybe you noticed me at school? I always try to be as close to you as possible. Sometimes I wonder, whether you have any magical or mesmerizing abilities, that have fascinated me. I think of you so much. I often can't focus on my studies because I no longer concentrate on anything other than you for every second that I am breathing, and even in my dreams, I often see you as a mesmerizing angel.

I'm so obsessed with you. I often imagine how we both hold hands together, and go to some beautiful place, maybe a park, and sit on a bench by the city lake and watch the ducks that float in it, and then I realize that you are not here with me right now.

My Feelings toward you are like an addiction or a curse because I can't get you out of my head, I've wanted to come to approach you very often but, most of the time, I'm ashamed and restrained. I am standing like a frozen statue in such moments because I think you might not like me. After all, I am not as attractive as other guys. My heart would break into fragile tiny glass crumbs if you rejected me.

I'm still dreaming of that Halloween event, when I was so happy to be around you, even for a couple of dances and when we danced together, you were my ball Queen. I wanted to kiss you yesterday with all my heart on your tempting cherry red lips, and I know that they would be much sweeter than any cherry berries.

Remember how you tried to take off my mask? I couldn't reveal my face to you. After all, I feel like I have no hope to be with you because I'm an ugly outcast, whose destiny is to stay alone forever but, maybe there's a small hope, that you'll be able to give me a little chance and please my empty heart.

- Maggie, I want to ask you, would you like to go on a date with me?

Of course, I'm afraid you won't like me but, please give me this opportunity to meet you. I'll be waiting for you on Monday in the school's stadium after your math class, which I know is your favorite. I'm willing to wait even until late at night, while I'm a little scared for you to discover who I am but, I can't wait any longer. See you soon! I will be waiting for you with red roses; please come...

Your Secret Admirer

Vincent wanted to hear Maggie's voice, so he entered

her phone number on his cell phone and felt how he started to get very nervous when he heard the first beep.

- Yes, I'm listening, - Maggie said in a hollow, slightly hoarse voice. Vincent didn't answer and continued to listen to her voice.

- Hello! Who am I talking to? Maggie asked loudly and realized something must have gone wrong because no one replied, so she hung up.

Vincent grabbed a black jacket, that had dropped on his chair, pulled on the hood, and put on his sports shoes, while was holding a red envelope with a heart on it, that had written with a gold ink pen on top. He ran into the kitchen, which smelled of bacon and omelettes, and put his hand on Eva's shoulder. She didn't turn in his direction but continued to stir the small sugar grains in her steaming teacup with a teaspoon.

- I will not eat today but, I got to go for a run now! Vincent said with a smile on his face while hiding the folded letter behind him.

- What was that creaking noise behind you? Eva asked and turned to Vincent and put on her huge glasses.

- It's a letter addressed to a particular person.

- You should better sit at home and study, rather than wander around. You have such bad grades, that you may not finish school.

- I will not be away for long, when I return home, I will start studying immediately.

- Where are you going?

- I'm going for a walk, - Vincent said while was closing the door behind him.

- Wait! Eat something! - Eve said as she sipped her tea and inhaled its pungent aroma.

* * *

- I'm finally here, and I see that there is the number eleven on the wall of the wooden board house, - Vincent thought and approached the mailbox and threw the letter into the angular mailbox, next to which in the muddy ground stood a wooden owl and looked with its red, glassy eyes, towards the bare birch. The tiny house was surrounded by forest, and its green plaster resembled a fairy-tale cottage. In several places, the orange tiles were missing from the roof and had left un-obstructed holes, while a black fume was smoking through the chimney. Vincent turned his head because of a hollow sound. He saw how a man holding in his hand a black cat opened the door of the house and then threw out the fluffy kitten into the yard.

- What are you doing here? Huh? - Called out loudly the man, who looked like he was in his forties, quite pleasant and approached Vincent closer. He had long, dark hair tied in a thin ponytail and slippers on his feet. A strong smell of alcohol came from the man's breath, and a considerable surge of anger was felt, which had painted his whole face in very red tones.

- What are you doing here? I am asking again! Are you the

little bastard, who stole my daughter's bike? The man's eyes widened as he asked again.

- Uhh ... I'm Maggie's classmate. Does she live here?

- What do you need from her? She's not home!

- I just wanted to give her the class's field trip plan.

- Field trip? Doesn't a teacher have to deal with it?

- Well, a teacher told me to do it! Please, tell me when Maggie will be at home?

- When she will be, then she will be! I don't know! While swaying against the loose fence of metal gratings, the man waved his hand at a man passing by and was holding a large bottle of vodka in his hands and greeted him as an old friend.

- Hey, come on in! I've been looking out the window from time to time, waiting for you to come. I've been waiting for you for an hour already.

- Couldn't come sooner, - the man smiled and exposed a few teeth in his mouth.

Vincent turned his back on both men and walked down the small path into the forest paddock, which was the straightest way to get home.

* * *

It was a Monday morning, and as the first birds started chirping, Vincent opened his eyes slowly. Vincent had set the clock one hour earlier the night before to have more time to prepare in advance for everything, that had been planned because today was a special day. He brushed his teeth and sleeked his relaxed hair back with his hair gel; after that, he looked like a miniature version of Dracula.

- No, that looks terrible! - he broke the sleek hairstyle and blew some perfume from a blue bottle that Eva had given him on his birthday, he would never have chosen such a sweet fragrance.

- This time should work because I will meet a sweet girl, - Vincent thought.

- What should I wear? I have to dress in an alternative style, just like she, - Vincent said while was looking in the mirror and reached his fingers to take a black shirt with a skull and a motorcycle from the top shelf of the closet. He put a chain on one of his pockets, chose to wear trousers with torn patterns, and put the red roses in the paper bag he bought yesterday, which smelled quite pleasant when he put them close to his stumpy nose.

- Red as her lips! - Vincent said while was smelling the roses and kissed one of the bright flowers.

Vincent jumped in the school bus, and he felt so happy, that the corners of his lips rose on their own. From time to time, Vincent looked at the bus window, where his face shone like in a mirror, so he decided to brush up his thick, messy hair. Vincent accidentally tapped the woman's shoulder with his sharp elbow sitting next to him. She immediately peeked pompously at Vincent from top to bottom, then continued to browse her creaking magazine. When Vincent approached the final stop, he noticed the sun's long rays breaking through the pine trees and illuminating the winding road in a light green color.

Vincent entered the classroom and sat down in his usual place by the window. As the hours passed by, he looked out the window and was watching how the gardener was grabbing the fallen yellow leaves and was dropping them into a large pile, while the wind that existed outside had its own game and it tore the neatly formed bank and twisted the small leaves in a tiny swirl.

The teacher was standing at the blackboard and was drawing diagrams with white chalk, which reminded city towers. She noticed how Vincent was dreamily looking outside the window and, in a loud voice, interrupted his world of thoughts:

- Vincent, please come and solve this task!

Vincent took slow steps to the board and was staring at one point for a long time as if he saw foreign and very distant language. Many words in the task were unseen, and he could not put their meaning together in one thought.

- In the future, you will be sweeping the streets! Sit down! - The teacher said and fit her square glasses from her nose.

As someone opened the door, a familiar face poked through the small gap and said with a wide smile, - Vincent, you have to go to the doctor with me now, - Eva said and waved her hand in his direction. Vincent walked out the door through the classroom at mighty speed and looked at Eva in confusion.

- What are you doing here? Where do we have to go? - Vincent asked in surprise.

- I made an appointment at the dentist! - Eva said insistently.

- I'm not going anywhere because I have intended other vital plans! - Vincent roared.

- Do you even understand how difficult it was for me to arrange a visit with the primary doctor? I have been waiting for several months in a row.

- Then go by yourself!

- Vincent, you're a minor, and I'm raising you. I am your mother, and you have to listen to me!

- No, you are not my mother and never will be! - Vincent said as he was about to return to the classroom.

- And so, this is how you reward me for all my efforts! What have I done to you? - Eva said while was sobbing and pulled out a checkered handkerchief from her handbag's pocket.

- Well, let's do as you want, if that is going to make you feel better!

As Eva entered the empty parking lot of the polyclinic and parked her car in front of the thick, yellow maple, a gray lady was pushing her trolley and crossed the asphalted road. Her back was so bent that it looked like she was going at a ninety-degree angle, and from time to time, she stopped and rested for a bit. At the front door's stood a small, skinny girl with a dirty mouth and curly hair. She looked after the baby in the pram, who was sweetly sleeping while two little boys were running around her. Their clothes were soiled with dirty stains, and the rays of his trousers had thoroughly torn along his seams for one of the youngest boys. As they passed the young children,

Eva didn't pay any attention to them and energetically opened the door' of the white, huge, glazed building; when they entered the long corridor of the hospital, a bright light shone in their eyes and was illuminating the farthest corner of the building. Vincent sat down on the purple wooden chair placed by the mosaic window next to a woman looking around nervously while rocking her feet. He looked at the front door and noticed the sign 'Psychiatrist' had written on it.

The woman sitting next to him turned her head to Vincent's side and began to tell him, how she had flooded her lower neighbor, and after a short time, she repeated the same incident but, when she saw that Vincent wasn't paying the slightest bit of attention to her, she turned her head to the other side and began to talk to the man next to her, who was staring at one point with his mouth open. The only woman who paid attention to her was a beautiful young woman who was sitting in a corner, frustrated and so sad, that her heart seemed to have broken into small pieces. From time to time, the young woman looked at the woman who was talking and nodded in agreement.

- You didn't tell me, that we will go to the psychiatrist. You said we would go to the dentist, - Vincent looked at Eva, who was sitting next to him, and as she opened her mouth to answer, then a bald man in a white robe and with round glasses came out.

- Vincent Kronberg, please! - he called him inside.

Before entering the office, Vincent first noticed a withered flower in a flowerpot standing alone in the corner of a windowsill. The doctor called him to sit down in the seat as he flipped through a white, shiny folder.

- Tell me, why did you come here?

- We came so that you can see what's wrong with Vincent. There's something wrong with him, - Eva said in a severe tone.

- Vincent, what do you think? Why did your mom bring you here?

- Well, she's not my birth mother but, my foster mother. Well, I think she sent me here because I'm a little bit weird. After all, I don't have any friends, and I don't speak in class.

- Yes, he doesn't speak in class, - Eva added.

- But what if I start saying that my classmates are fools? I am not to blame for that.

- Vincent, how are you talking?

- What? I'm just telling you the truth! You wanted me to come here!

- Well, I'll check him to see if he's okay. Vincent, look at this pen! - The psychiatrist took a pen in his hand and placed it in front of his face.

Following the pen movements, the man moved the pen from side to side, while watching Vincent's eyes movements.

- He is fine; you shouldn't come to me but, a psychologist. I don't check the kind of problems you have come to me.

- Goodbye, I have a lot of work to do! Such a long line is waiting outside.

- Goodbye! We will make an appointment with a psychologist, - Eva said with a smile but, when she turned to leave the office, a gray gloom appeared on her face.

<h1 style="text-align:center">9</h1>

The long-awaited meeting with Maggie

Vincent had been standing under the big, ancient oak for half an hour and was hiding from the fine rain, which poured on the long grass stalks like morning dew, and the sun's rays broke out of the light gray clouds and were gleaming in the tiny raindrops.

Vincent leaned against the softly mossed oak trunk and didn't notice that he had smeared his light jeans with huge, muddy stains. Every few minutes, he looked at the clock, and it seemed that time was running like it had wings of the wind. He wondered what to say to Maggie or what to ask but, no thought came to his mind.

- Fifteen minutes have passed but, she has not yet arrived. Maybe she hasn't read my letter? - Vincent began to struggle while was thinking about her, and he took a few steps, here and there and didn't notice, that behind him had come the girl and was standing like a still ghost, - She had been watching his every move, then suddenly turned and walked away, when Vincent noticed her, he started to run to her and exclaimed:

- Wait, Maggie!

The girl stopped but, didn't turn to him, just continued to stand as if she had been glued to the ground. Vincent took a quick step in front of her and pulled out a red rose from his crumpled paper bag. The flower heads of roses had slightly bent but, anyway, he carefully placed them in her hand, then he lifted his slanted head and smiled and felt how his cheeks flushed in bright red color. Vincent was too shy to dare look into her eyes but, when he finally raised his head, he noticed that she had a blue eye.

- Thank you! It seemed that the letter from you was a joke but, now it looks like it is not, - she smiled artificially.

- Do you have time to talk with me a little bit? - Vincent asked with a nervous smile as his voice awkwardly broke.

- Yes, I have some time.

Vincent couldn't stop looking at Maggie's deep green and crystal-clear eyes, and while he was staring at her beautiful face, he came closer to her and ran with his shoulder into the spruce in front of him.

- Be careful! Maybe tell me better, how do you know my home address? - Maggie asked.

- Your classmate gave me your address.

- Who exactly?

- I must not reveal it to you because we are good childhood friends.

- So, it was you who danced with me at the ball?

- Yes, it was me. Did you like to dance with me?

- Why do you stare at me like this all the time?

- Excuse me but, I don't want to offend you, and I don't want to bother you but, I need to know who hurt you? Why do you have an eye flick?

- I don't want to talk about it.

- Well, please tell me! Maybe I can help you?

- As I said, I don't want to talk about it.

- Tell me, was that your father? - Vincent came closer and stroked Maggie's face with the palm of his hand.

- Why would my father beat me? - Maggie pushed Vincent's hand away.

- Because I know he likes alcohol. Did he hit you?

- Are you stupid? How dare you talk about my father like this! You don't know him at all!

- I'm sorry, please, I didn't want to offend you, just when I went to the house where you live and threw the letter in your mailbox, your father came out, and I noticed, that he was drunk and also I saw, that some strange guy came to visit him with a bottle of vodka in his hands.

- Please tell me, did your father hurt you?

- That's not normal! Maybe you're already watching me with binoculars? My father is the best father anyone could have, and he is not an alcoholic. Yes, he likes to drink but, you don't know what he's been through. If you want to know, by the way, the person who had hit me was Wendy because I was kissing her boyfriend at a Halloween party, even though I didn't know, that he wasn't a single guy.

- It happened because you chose to pay attention to the wrong guy; if you ever wanted, I would have always been there for you, and anything like that would never even happen.

- Then you think I'm guilty of everything? Then it turns out that you support her beating me.

- No, I don't support it but, I think you shouldn't have even looked at that type of man. He loves only himself.

Maggie looked at Vincent sternly, took his palm, and gave back the roses he had previously given. He grabbed her by the elbow and didn't let her go.

- Sorry, please! I'm so sorry! I didn't mean to offend you! I just wanted to help you.

- Let me go! I don't know you!

- That's okay, we are here to get to know each other and maybe even become something more.

The gift of roses slipped from Vincent's hand, and he strangled Maggie's arm, unable to let her go; one more time, he looked at her with despair in his eyes while didn't notice, that he had crushed the thick blooms of flowers. Vincent tried to kiss the girl but, she tilted her face, turned her head, and pushed him so hard, that he fell to the muddy ground. The boy watched as she began to run away at a very high speed. She tore a large hole in her black tights and scratched her knee to blood when she had run past the open gate doors from which several wires had slipped out.

- When can we meet again? Maybe tomorrow? Don't run away, please! Vincent shouted as loudly as he could, then pulled his cell phone out of his pocket and called Maggie but, she didn't pick up the phone, so he decided to text her and pushed his back against the tree.

I want to apologize to you, really from the bottom of my heart. Please forgive me for everything that I did wrong. I hope you will give me another chance and agree to meet me. Dear sunshine, I will be waiting for you every day after class lessons in the school's stadium, where we met today. Vincent

- I'm not interested in you, so it would be better if you would leave me alone, - Maggie replied in a text message.

- Please give me a chance! Ever since I saw you, I have become crazy! I swear I'll commit suicide if you don't want to talk to me anymore.

- We can be friends if you want but, nothing more.

- I will never be able to look at you as a friend. Maybe if you don't like me now, you will like me eventually. Please, give me just one opportunity to meet you again.

- No, I'm blocking your phone number! Goodbye! Hopefully, you won't bother me anymore!

- Please, please, please, please, don't do this! I love you! Please give me a chance!

* * *

Vincent's diary (7 years later)

Hi, I'm sitting alone in my quiet room, and I'm listening to the crows creak behind the window, while they are flying from one tree branch to another. I hadn't written anything in seven years. No one is home right now but, here I am. I have a computer on the table with my unfinished bachelor's thesis. I have to study a lot but, my thoughts are still flying, and I can't concentrate at all because I still think of the girl with crystal green eyes, who left me alone, even though seven years had passed. Sometimes, when I miss her, I look at her phone number, and you can't even imagine, how many times I had wanted to write her but, I always stop myself because I realize that it's pointless. As far as I know, she went to study in college but, I don't know exactly what. Unfortunately, she is now together with some handsome man who dresses like her, all in black and is tattooed. He has an alternative type, just like herself.

I still get heartache every time I recall that time when we met at that damn school's stadium. I had waited under the big oak where I first met her, after my school's hours for months, every single day but, she never came, and the children who went home through the school's stadium had been memorizing me, and when they passed by, they always looked back at me thoroughly and sometimes laughed at me. All these peals of laughter shrilled my heart like sharp knife stabs, just like the sensitive eyes, when the whole school knew about my case with Raivo but, what can I say? I had always been an outcast in my class anyway. I still remember that incident, when I met in a shop my childhood's friend Niklav, he had approached by some guy he knew from my school who I didn't know, and he asked him:

- Why are you talking to him at all? Everyone is making fun of him! He is nothing! He is just a wall!

I didn't want to fight at that moment, so I just went home that day. I had a feeling as if a heavy stone had fallen on my heart which was impossible to throw away. One day I wanted to tear up all the pictures of my class, that had lain in the very bottom in the drawer of the closet. I found them when I had been looking at the old diplomas. I felt so bad when I saw their faces because of their disgusting grins and evil narrow eyes. I just wanted to vomit.

I had broken any contact with my previous life, however, I only contacted Eva sometimes. It seems, that she a little bit misses me, maybe because she is very lonely and now that we no longer live together, she has calmed down. I don't know why we couldn't live in a friendly way earlier because life is so short but, now our relationships are entirely settled, just like a calm sea with little white waves.

Do I miss the old house I grew up in? Yes, I miss my childhood home, and one day I went there and saw, that it was utterly destroyed, the windows had broken, the walls of the house had been covered with graffiti, and the entrance door had burned. I couldn't walk inside the house because I felt too scared to see the crime, that had done to my sweet old childhood home but, most of all, I didn't want to get sad again. Upon entering the small town, the old memories had flashed like in a movie where I could vividly see my mother's face and how she baked pancakes in the mornings or weeded flowers in the garden. I don't know, maybe I fell in love with that girl like a crazy fool because in fact, I missed my mother very much all this time, more than anything in the world, and she a little bit reminded me of her.

I still think about my mom every single dammit day. Where has she been all this time? What has happened to her? And still, now I haven't received any answers. I had walked all over the hometown while I was showing my mom's pictures. I asked people on the street, at the bus stops, and in the shops, if they had seen my mom but, they didn't know anything about her, so I decided to hire a private investigator for the money I earned working as a gardener in the summer. I must say that he hadn't answered anything specific to me for about six months when I called and asked him for my answers but, I'll hope forever and still look forward to some news from him...

There is something else I want to tell you about, what happened after ninth grade. After the ninth grade, as I had agreed, I moved to live with my father. In the beginning, he paid me a lot of attention and spent most of his free time with me; so, to speak, he tried to make up for the lost time. We always went somewhere on weekends and excursions with my sister and his wife. Still, over time he became more and more immersed in his work, and sometimes, I didn't even see him for several days because he stayed in the office until late at night and, as one might say, lived literally like a fish in the water, at work. His wife remained completely jealous and didn't believe, that he was at work until late at night, so she demanded more and more attention but, he chose his job because, as he said, he is a workaholic and would only rest once he died.

Although I didn't think that, the real-life should be like this because he had already died in his way. He saw nothing else than his work desk and when he came home, he was angry and tired. He always had dark blue rings under his eyes, and he used to drink a lot of coffee to ward off his sweet yawns.

What was my relationship with his wife? At first, she was friendly but, internally it always seemed, that it was painful to her to look at me because I had bornt when they were both married, and now I was at their home twenty-four hours a day and seven days a week. Sometimes I didn't understand her ability to forgive him? She often sat in her room and watched television, all the possible shows in a row; sometimes, it seemed that she wasn't interested in anything else, including her daughter. The girl was rarely home because she spent all her time in sports training and usually went to races on holidays but, no matter what, she was always smiling when she saw me, and it looked like she wanted to say, that there were no problems with her life.

I sometimes wondered how, in such a wealthy family, such a lovely, friendly, and always smiling girl had grown up, who although had spoiled with all the luxury in her life. She is natural sunshine and not an arrogant little brat. I often missed her because the house without her seemed very quiet. I rarely saw her, just like our father but, when she was home, she used to knock on my room doors and ask how I was doing. My sister is very social, and she has no problem with meeting new people; a few times, we even went to discos together, and she always greeted a lot of people, as if she knew half of the city. On one occasion, when she had been drunk, she admitted to me that the first time she saw me, she was a little bit internally jealous of me because she knew she would need to share her father's attention, and she also said that sometimes she didn't know if she liked guys or girls better, or both. Her mother became thoroughly angry when she had noticed that the parties started to ruin her training and competition results but, her father didn't care; he was too busy with his job.

I almost forgot to tell you about my new class when I was studying in high school! After the ninth grade, I changed my school, and my new sister helped me change my image for the better and get into school. The first week I had been closely watched by everyone, as the class was mostly made up of students who had studied together from the first grade and everyone knew each other but, I wasn't the only new one, there were five more new students. I made friends with one of them, and all through high school, we had been staying by each side to side together; there had also been some unpleasant people but, they didn't bother me much in general; we were coexisting together just fine. We always helped each other, and I even got better marks.

School time passed quickly, probably because I had made my first real friend, now we have each gone our way, we live far from each other.

Although my grades after high school had greatly improved, I still couldn't pass the drawing exam well enough to get an architecture place in university, so my father helped me with tuition fees, and I completed my bachelor's degree. In a way, my father and I have chosen similar professions, he is a furniture designer but, I will be an architect in a few years but, who knows, maybe I will be even more successful in his field than he is. Without my father, I would never have been able to pay those vast sums, what the school demands but, they are only pennies for him. I sometimes think, and really can't understand, why he didn't try to help me and my mom earlier, when we were almost dying of poverty and hunger. Was my mother *so proud to refuse to see him and get him out of my life and not accept any help? And if so, then it hadn't been fair to me at all. Did my father regret leaving my mother and me? He could fight for me more! Then who is telling the truth, and who is lying? I don't know. I had forgiven him, and I am grateful that he found me and that he tried to recover all the lost time because he was genuinely showing his care and love for me, no matter what mean things Eva had said about him.*

My diary, I'm going to go to bed now; the crows behind the window are now silent, probably because it's already utterly dark in such a short time. I had set the alarm clock early in the morning to continue to write my bachelor's thesis again. Looking forward to seeing you soon, I am saying that with bright eyes!

Vincent

The clock with a loud noise struck the eighth hour of the morning, and suddenly the phone rang with a loud noise. Vincent rubbed his sleepy eyes, reached his hand towards the drawer of the wooden chest, grabbed the cell phone, and without looking at who the caller was, put the phone to his ear and said...

- Yes, I'm listening.

- Hello, am I talking to Vincent Kronberg?

- Yes, with Vincent.

- The private investigator calling here, I have information about your mother. Tell me, when could we meet?

- Please, tell me what you know by phone. I need to know everything right now.

- Of course, as you wish, usually such things I discuss in real life. It is that I had found out that in the village where your mother had previously lived when she was a child, there is a tomb with her name, last name, and the exact date of birth. Vincent, do you hear me?

- I don't believe it? When did she die?

- She died a year ago when she disappeared. I am very sorry.

- How did she die?

- I'm sorry but, I don't know anything about that.

- How did you find out?

- I have access to a database.

Vincent felt how a sea of tears was flowing into his eyes and as he hysterically fainted on the ground and hit the floor with his palms but, the pain didn't subside. He wanted to merge with the earth, not to feel the pain of this life repeatedly.

- I have hit my limits, - Vincent stood up and strolled to the kitchen, and took a bottle of brandy from the top shelf that his sister had given him on his birthday. He poured the strong drink into a glass of juice and drank it empty. He felt how it was burning his throat. Still, he continued to drink and drink until he felt his mind start to disengage and everything around him began to spin in a fast carousel but, even when he closed his eyes, everything in mind was continuing its swirling swirl. When the bottle had emptied, he went for the next bottle, and when he drank it, he couldn't stand anymore, so he crawled to the edge of the sofa while was leaning against its edge. Vincent poured another glass one more time but, his hands didn't listen, just like in his childhood, when he had learned to eat with a spoon, it always fell out of his hand. A slippery glass with a large bang fell to the ground and shattered into small, sharp fragments, and his whole body collapsed directly on top of the most brilliant piece of glass and stabbed his neck. Everything around him was surrounded by one thick mist, and as his vision had darkened, he didn't feel pain any longer, nor bleeding wounds from glass that had broken and had pierced his eyes and neck like sharp needles. He fell into a deep, dark, and lonely sleep when he heard a whisper...

10

The unusual flight to the place of love

Silent whispers became louder and louder. Some strong force made Vincent sit up slowly. It was against his will, and the body began to move by itself as if some mystical magnet had triggered it. When he turned his head to the right, the man was terrified because he saw how his body lay motionless. In the middle of the room, white rays had broken through the ceiling and reminded a morning fog glowing in the sun. Vincent noticed an unfamiliar white silhouette walking around, making light rays around the room, and quietly whispering something.

- That's a ghost!!! - the young man said in a shaky voice, as he tried to escape away as far as possible while he had a panic attack but, he couldn't because his whole body wasn't moving, and his legs were like being complete with lead. Nothing happened as he wanted, and, most importantly, he couldn't operate his body any longer as he wanted. Vincent couldn't get up from the floor; he seemed utterly separated from his body.

The mist-shaped woman was slipping up at tremendous speed and pointed one of her hands towards the terrified man and pointed with her gestures slowly and calmly to a beam of light with her other hand but, it didn't help Vincent to calm down.

Vincent tried to wake up from this mystical dream but, this strange reality continued. Vincent felt how he had been detaching from his sleeping body and was about twenty centimeters above the floor's surface. He began to slide on top of the woman's silhouette but, by the time he had slipped through her, Vincent realized that he had either dreamed or had gone through another soul.

The man had dragged into the white beam of fog with some inexplicable strength, which was constantly moving and somewhat recalled a waterfall. Vincent blended into the thick fog, and he didn't see the silhouette of his hands, legs, shoulders, or stomach any longer. He saw nothing but a prism with white light. He was flying towards the light beam at a very high speed, just like the most powerful space rocket. The bright rays of light, like a white inclusive tunnel, began to narrow, and a mountain in the color of halva appeared in from of his eyes. He was flying directly towards it, just like the fastest eagle, and it seemed like he was about to crash into it. His foggy silhouette soared and flew over the mountain but then began to fall sharply down while he was flying over bright green fields. Vincent's hazy shape began to slow down and briefly stopped at a valley where all the houses looked the same and reminded white cubes. He looked at the buildings and once again continued to glide through the small village, which was empty with no living souls in it. He felt scared of the unknown and that his body was moving by itself and that he couldn't control it anymore but, at the same time, he felt free because he could fly at such a tremendous speed, realizing that one part of his life was over. He was still alive but, only in a different form.

- Energy is not lost and does not re-emerge, it only turns from one form of energy to another or moves from one body to another, - as he moved closer to the winding, small stream, he remembered the law of physics, he had heard at school and realized that at this point, this law, was really and truly alive. A small, antique wooden boat reminded of Viking times and had moored on the riverbank; in it, a white mist woman was standing, that he had seen in previously his room. She smiled kindly and invited him to get on the boat but, Vincent didn't want to go into the unknown and tried with all his might to slip past her. For the first time, his volatile silhouette obeyed and passed directly above the woman's head and reached a yellowish, moss-covered bridge. Vincent stopped abruptly and felt a little confused, when he saw a city whose buildings were a little bigger, than those he had seen before but, they were all made of concrete, and all were the same. Vincent wanted to take a closer look at the city but felt that some kind of force started to control his body again. As slowly as possible, he slipped into the dark brown boat. In front of the massive ship stood a tall man with a long nose, coal-black hair, and warm brown eyes, he looked grave and didn't smile, yet his eyes were good-natured.

- Where are we going? - Vincent asked when the boat started to move away from the shore.

- It's time for you to get to know a new place! - quietly blew the man in the black robe and put his elongated hood on his head.

- What place is it? What's going on? Am I still alive or just dreaming? - Vincent screamed aloud.

- Wait, you'll see by yourself! - said the boatman and began to drive the ancient boat.

- Answer me! I want to know where I am? Let me out! - Vincent yelled desperately and tried to pull off the boatman's hood but, touching it, his hand went through his silhouette.

The boat rapidly approached the sun-blaspheming sea, whose waves moved gently and moved the boatman's long robe in motion. The ship continued its course further into the deep staples of the sea, which was so quiet and calm that Vincent couldn't hear even the slightest sound of the wind outside. The peace of the sea brought peace to his soul, and he stopped breathing fast, and his chest rose more slowly, and he calmed down.

In the middle of the sea, a tropical island emerged from the bottom of the sea; in its state, it boasted the leafy tops of the ruby-green palm trees, which stood peacefully on the shore and invited them to visit it amicably.

- There's an island! Is this where we are going? - the man pointed his index finger towards the island and asked in amazement but, he received no response from the boatman.

- There is somebody! - Vincent watched as several silhouettes of people playing volleyball on the island's shores. It seemed that there were no problems or the slightest sadness in their present lives, that could overshadow this delight.

- What a strange feeling! - said Vincent and opened his mouth, while was looking at the flashing gold waterfall, the most beautiful he had ever seen. The magical waterfall was transparent and clear, it called for getting closer and merging with it altogether. There were three people near the waterfall, they all gleefully were floundering and jumping around it; one of them clutched his head while his shoulders of the whiff foamy water were washing him gently. All these people were full of happiness and enjoyed the aura and presence of love. Vincent, felt like hungry for honey or thirsty for a sip of water in the middle of the desert, wanted to get closer to this mystical water formation, so he put both feet over the edge of the boat and jumped to the bottom of the sea. Vincent didn't feel whether the sea was warm or cold, and it was a strange and unusual feeling, nor did he want to eat or sleep and, most importantly, he was no longer sad or worried because the most important thing was to get closer to the waterfall.

Vincent swam closer to the other people, while was waving both hands; when they noticed him, they splashed the water with happiness and invited him to join them in the joyful dance to the swirling waterfall. These people, who knew neither the grief nor the dark aches in the gorge, were laughing loudly, and their laughter sounded like the first bells of the morning sunshine.

- What's the secret of this waterfall? - Vincent asked and reached out to a stream of water that was radiant in his secret.

It's the source of origin, a symbol of life; with it, you can be reborn and lose all sadness in it. Souls become crystal clear and full of energy; they are loved and understood here because this water heals and cleanses, bringing joy and happiness. Broken souls, tie here as a magnet and purges from all the negatives, - said the boatman and smiled with loving eyes.

- I have to go now to meet a new traveller because I feel he's very close to the valley's river. Goodbye and let the light be with you!

Vincent nodded and closed his eyes, his intrusive thoughts scattered into the sounds of waterfall rustling in its brightness.

- My parents didn't love me and left me alone when I was born but, now it doesn't matter, - said the young man and was holding a white shell in one of his hands.

- No one wanted to be friends with me at school, and later when I met my wife, she went to another man; I loved her more than anything in the world but, she broke my heart and left only an empty shell but, now my heart is whole with peace. I couldn't stand the sadness in my heart anymore, so I tried to commit suicide but, my mother arrived just at that moment when I had put a rope around my neck. The shame I felt in front of her, I still remember, - in a calm and low tone, determined the man who was in his best shape ever, while his light curly hair was shining as they had made of gold. He sat on a sizeable canny stone near the surface of golden honey water and started to smile with his broadest smile possible.

- My house had burned down with me but, as you can see, I'm alive and more alive than ever! Said the third man and hit Vincent's shoulder, standing with his back to the waterfall stream and inviting him to stand under the waterfall.

I know what you have experienced because I see your life when I close my eyes. I know that you had many painful moments in your life but, as you can see, it has only made you stronger and brighter, even though the black pain whirlpools had dragged you into its nets. Do you know that you're free of your pain now?

- If I'm dead, please tell me more about my mother? - Vincent asked with deep pain in his eyes.

- She lives on Earth, and her path will still go a long way. When you were little, she had been deprived of her mother's rights because she had addiction problems, just as you used to quench the pain in the bottle, so she soothed her pain too. On a day when she wasn't home, she was so intoxicated that she couldn't even come home and fell asleep nearby at a small white church. A woman who knew her was passing by and recognized her when she was walking to work in the early morning and knew you were home alone. Your mom is broken right now because she's alone, and you've left Earth. She's crying right now, and a sea has already formed from her tears. Your mother loves you but, she was broken since childhood and therefore couldn't take proper care of you because the burden of pain was more substantial than the desire to live and dream. This feeling took over the desire to rejoice about the first rays of the morning's sun, the silver smile of the moon, the life-full sprouts of the spring, or the mystical star map of the night in which our stories, each one's stories, are recorded.

- If she was alive all this time, why didn't she ever try to find me? - the red-haired man asked.

She often thought of you but, she started to have mental issues because of her drinking problems, which put her in a mental hospital. No one told you anything because they didn't do their job and were indifferent; even Eva knew everything but, didn't want you to make her visit all the time. Human negligence, Vincent! - determined the man and wiped the tears of Vincent, which, like raindrops, drained along his cheeks:

- It's time to forgive, and it's time to wash away the old past; even though time doesn't exist here, you can be as young as ever again but, not you because you had been already young, when you poisoned yourself, right up to the very last drop, and this is what happened but, it doesn't matter here anymore.

Vincent realized, that at this point, he would give anything just to return to his old life, then he would find his mother, and he would hug her firmly.

- I want to meet my mother more than anything in the world and tell her that I love her, and I have been missing her all these years! Mom, if you hear me now, then know that I love you! It has been hard for me without you, without your good words in difficult moments of life, your embrace, when

I was lonely and sad, and your soft, loving voice, which always sounded in such a gentle, airy hue. Mother's low voice is still in my memory, as her warm smile and deep eyes. I want to see you but, I can't because I drank my whole life from just one bottle and pills because I didn't see the point of life anymore. My life was so empty and lonely because you haven't been there for so long...

So many times, I was angry and hated you because I thought you'd left me. Where are you, my mummy?

Vincent felt how his body was embarking on its flight, and he was again out of control. At the same time, the next journey had just begun. He gradually moved away from the tropical island and continued to fly over the glimmering sea until he noticed substantial rock formations on the first horizon, that looked like a teal tower rifted in large parts. Vincent flew like a bird, and as he approached the first huge rock, he noticed, that the sea had been covered with a white veil of fog. A thick layer of mist surrounded Vincent's body and saw no more himself or the ancient stone formations. Rocks reminded stately pine trees, so firmly with their roots, they had grown into the ground, that even the strongest storm could not pull them out of the depths of the water.

The pine silhouettes had become smaller, and Vincent realized, that he was rising higher and higher. The veil of the thick fog quickly vanished and revealed its loneliness; peacefully quiet darkness had hugged it in a long coat. The colors of the night constantly changed from gray to dark purple and from dark purple to dark green, while all the colors mixed in one ball formed a long tunnel. Vincent slowly approached the dark tunnel through which he saw the light shining at the end of it, which became brighter, and its glow recalled the brightest bridge of the sun's rays or the shimmering silver of the moon's glow.

This beauty instilled peace and a feeling that everything would be fine wherever this path ended. Vincent realized, he was dead and will not be back in his previous life but, more than anything, he didn't want everything to end on the other side of the tunnel...

Thoughts of the absence of his existence frightened him - to not be anything and anywhere in this strange dream. His questions grew more robust, and as soon as possible, Vincent wanted to know the answers, that had in his mind and what was on the other side of a glowing silver light tunnel.

The dark coat became more expansive, and the first thing Vincent noticed in the distance was a huge, white round bullet shimmering like the brightest crystal. The beam bundle had been covered with red ruby stones and surrounded by bluish light water drops formations. Vincent flew into the indescribable artwork with great admiration, and in front of his eyes appeared the gleaming bluish dust of space. He seemed to fly in a completely different matter, where the laws of physics and gravity no longer exist. The bluish dust touched his pale silhouette but didn't go through him, they were soft, like down feathers, and their touches slightly set his airy body silhouette in motion.

At the end of the tunnel, the darkness had disappeared

altogether, and the bluish beam surrounded Vincent and kindly called in his new world, and what, he understood was that:

- This is my new home!

Vincent smiled and opened his arms wide open while was trying to catch the flashing dust. He inhaled a deep breath and realized that he was rapidly approaching the huge bright bullet, that looked like a completely different planet which was very different from Earth where he had spent twenty-four years of his life. The blue light road veil became more transparent, and the view opened to a glittering white planet covered with diamond-like crystals and red rubies, with blood-red rivers flowing through it.

- Why are these rivers blood red? - Vincent asked with his mouth open and frowned in dismay.

Although his journey on this new planet seemed to end, he was wrong because, as with some magnetic pull-up force, he was continuing his flight toward a miniature gray planetary moon or stone.

Vincent's feet touched the hard surface, and his body heavily leaned forwards to the rapid landing, and he fell but, when he looked up a little, he noticed the silhouette of a man twice as tall, who had turned with his backside and had spread his hands like a bird. Vincent noticed, that he stood in his solitude without shoes on his feet and saw, that his hair was auburn, slightly curly, and right up to his shoulders. The unusual man had dressed in a new brownish outfit resembling a cotton robe.

Internally, he understood who this man was but, he didn't

want to say his name aloud because who knows his true character.

- I know who you are! - determined Vincent and felt his feeling of loneliness and pain coming from the pristine man but, although approached, he didn't turn his face towards Vincent but, with open arms, continued to stand and stare at the bluish twilight nebula.

For the first time in his life, his heart was poured in with as much love as ever. In its most immediate sense, the word love had quick alive, and it had been distributed by this tall and mighty man.

I am so happy that I have met you and can finally feel your infinite and warm love. Can I see your face?

Vincent realized that he may have made many mistakes in his life, that he regretted right now, and that he was deliberately turned his back on him in this saint's being. But still, why do I feel internally unconditional love from him? - A man thought.

- You're my child, don't worry about it, - the loving being said peacefully.

Vincent was a grown man but, realized that he was seen as the joyful small kid who had eaten cherries and had enjoyed all the little things that gave meaning to life, just as when his mom had hugged and had said a sweet word and when the sun had sweetly warmed and had smiled lightly:

- Child, keep on being happy!

- Why are you so sad? - with an irresistible eye gaze, asked Vincent

- Although I am young externally, I am already quite old internally and have seen and had heard everything, both good and evil. I had seen all the suffering and pain, as well as felt, had betrayal, and will never be able to forget it because I am immortal. I have to stand past the times! Sooner or later, with the new arrivals in the world, every person will start everything again from a white sheet and forget all the past pain. I can give you my love to heal your wounds because I feel you had suffered a lot and, often, felt lonely, just like me...

I hope that in this world, you will find peace. It is quite different here than on Earth but, don't be afraid because I think you will enjoy it here.

I I

The truths of life

- I want you to know that when you felt alone and abandoned, I'm there for you, - said the tall-built creature with the long hood in his head.

- So then why, if you saw it all from your side, why you couldn't help me and not only me but, there are so many people on the whole planet who are suffering and is in great poverty.

- Unfortunately, my dear Vincent, no matter how much I want to help you, I can't because only you can help yourself. Different situations in life are like cards that had predetermined from previous lives and their karma. Only with suffering and pain comes the struggle and the life lessons, with whom you become, quite a second and another person - better and stronger. Every person who comes to Earth is there

143

because of the Ego that had pulled themself away from the primordial source.

The one life, the second life, the third life, the cycle continues, whatever had described in the ancient books, the law of karma exists. Likewise, the sea of suffering peoples is causing by hurting each other because of the great Ego crawls, that come out of the ocean's depths. Only by learning and changing there is an opportunity to come back to the source, to all the great roots of the love of the universe, that can feed the soul of the spirit, - the tall man stretched out his hand and turned it towards Vincent, while a small ball of light was rushing towards them and flew with a silver luminosity very close to Vincent's face.

- What's this light? - Vincent asked and stepped back a little bit.

- It's the light of origin source! A tiny fraction of the very high and intelligent energy. Vincent, do you remember when you felt unfortunate?

- In my lifetime, I had often felt this way.

- But do you remember that time when you were running alone through the woods and looked up to heaven in despair, then that heavenly light came from me. I tried to show you a sign, that everything will be fine and that you have to keep on going and live your life to help others, give your love and become even more vital in your spirit as you have always been.

- Yes but, I want to know more about this world but, I'm afraid that, at any moment, you're going to disappear and it will turn out, that this is just a dream, - Vincent came closer to the ball of light and said it while was looking at it.

Vincent got up on his toes and tried to reach the shimmering ball, which was shining like a newly polished diamond, in all colors of the rainbow. He jumped and caught the small ball and watched how the bright light slipped out of his hand and flew back like a magnet to his actual owner - the man in a dark robe.

- Don't worry, I can't get away from you anywhere because a bit of me lives in you too. I am your inner strength and energy, the present moment.

- Tell me, please, something more about that! I wonder what we come from? I want to know everything!

- I can give you the answers but, you have to listen to me and try to memorize the nine truths I'm about to tell you.

- Hmmm. I have so many questions. May I know who you are? You remind me of a very sacred and religious person but, I don't know if it's you because I don't see your face. Could I look at you?

- I'm ready for your questions, ask for sure, even though I already know what you're going to ask!

YOU ARE INVULNERABLE!

- In several dimensions, there is created life and several worlds. You came from planet Earth - unique but, not the only one. Several worlds are similar but, now you see the Land of Astra in front of your eyes. The first ray of light has come and the first charge of energy from this place.

It all started with one mind, a sensual and invisible being, not made of any material and neither a person but, a whole - the supreme intelligence and wisdom that once a long time ago was utterly alone and very lonely and was covered into a pitch-black cloak of darkness. This ultimate, immaterial being wanted to feel love more than anything in the world, so it chose a new life path by dividing it into many small fragments. The small ray of light expanded only more significantly and more prominent from the darkness. The power and the strength of light were rolled into the shape of a large light ball and exploded while creating everything still alive. It also created an opportunity to have a life for you and be full of light and love.

You have walked your life path, you had suffered a lot but, at the same time, you had learned essential life lessons and become wiser. I see what hurt you the most, and it is because you lost your mother. You must know she's having an emotionally difficult time right now but, she's alive and thinks about you. She loves you, please never forget that!

Vincent, although you are emotionally still broken and was hurt as you had walked through the difficulties of life, just like a mirror that has broken into a million pieces, you have to understand, that you have become more robust and have said goodbye to your fragile, vulnerable body. Now your spirit is invulnerable and full of light. Our emotions injure but, also make us feel and love. You're invulnerable!

YOU STAND ABOVE YOUR PAIN, HUMILIATION, DESTRUCTIVE EMOTIONS

Emotions are a mirror of the soul and often more potent than the mind; they are written into the field of human information, or what you call on Earth - DNA. It shows us how we feel and helps us understand and adapt to any environment and survive but, not love because it is not an emotion; it comes from the inner essence and radiates like an opaque thread vibration. Light and love are the two main parts, that once were broken through the black darkness to create something as unique as the living world.

And my child, there is a critical meaning to understand, that life is an eternal process, and we are born first and then to die one day. Death is like a transition from one form of energy to another, and although we are standing here, star-studded, our time and life process have stopped. We are still breathing. However, we no longer need to sleep or eat because we are free from the fragile body, which is always on its crisp edge of existence, ready to collapse at any moment.

Vincent, all these fragile, harmful, and destructive emotions are over because now it doesn't matter anymore! You are stronger than the pain, abuse, humiliation, and bad people who have, hurt you because they are so small, fearful, and ignorant in their souls. A very long way to go to be fully able to forgive and see the highest essence of truth but, try to let go of pain and don't think about the bad anymore - about pain or fear because you are in My Realm of Light, where forgiveness is the primary healing to heal wounds.

YOU CAN BE EMOTIONALLY KILLED BUT, YOU WILL STILL BE ALIVE!

All living is eternal because it is a small fragment of the Great Light, the core of one large ball that fourteen billion years ago exploded. At the very beginning, the Ball of Light was a size of an atom but, the slight buzz of light could no longer be alone in the black pitch of darkness, so it decided to become all-inclusive with its great power of energy, living matter system. As the Great Light had exploded, the universe and galaxies were born and were creating a new home for the smaller and larger particles of Light, and one of these particles is you! Very small but, not as small as you think right now!

- I feel so tiny in front of such a large universe! - Vincent replied and looked towards the brightly shining planet and wondered what awaited him next.

- Remember, whatever happens to you, or it is physical pain, so great that you feel trapped in your body and emotionally devastated, and even when you no longer have the strength to get up from bed because you're immersed in the deepest darkness. It's essential to look up to heaven and try to remember the place you came from.

You weren't created with the intimacy of a woman and a man; you were born a long time ago, already when the Ball of Light had chosen, that it no longer wanted to be alone in his dark world but, decided to split into many particles, that was the moment when you were born too because you are part of the beginning!

No matter how life beats you or torments you, you always know that you cannot be destroyed because when life on Earth ends, you will still be alive, only in a different place, time, and airier form. After all, you have returned to the state of matter from which the whole origin comes. Energy can't be destroyed!

ALL GOOD THAT IS CREATED IS THE FRUIT OF LOVE

The moment the power of light had arisen, even though it was the size of a pin, there was so much love in it that it rained all over, and it could no longer keep those higher feelings within itself, which was the reason for creating a massive explosion of energy.

Love is meant for us to share it, so everything that happens in the world is strict as intended but, both pleasant and painful emotions allow us to look with clarity at Love - the highest feeling, the source of the power of Light.

When life is over, the Light will always pull the souls, as the strongest magnet, back to its faithful and true provenance but, those who abandon the path of love will end up in the infinite shadow of darkness.

It is essential to recognize that Love is the main reason that had led us to be born even if we didn't feel loved during our lifetime. Everything alive is a source of love!

- Do you remember when you were a little boy, you had so much energy, and sometimes you didn't understand where it's coming from? The answer is that you were alive before you had born, just as you are standing here at this moment. When you are born into a new world, of course, you don't remember anything but, always recall to yourself that you're just as old as the very provenance from which everything was created because you are a part of it. All living and environment were created from the same matter!

- I have to say that it's unnecessary to complain about things that haven't been in life but, others have had because it doesn't matter. Only love is essential because it is the primary source of strength and higher intelligence and the reason why we exist at all, without it we are nothing, only cold and infinite darkness, who has no feelings, who does not care about others or where you come from, - a miraculous creature determined by deep sighing.

Can you imagine people blaming the Great Light every day through prayers? Why don't I have anything? Why are others being gifted but, I don't? And the answer is that the Light gave your life and strength to stand up and do everything possible to live and receive your earned gifts, which can be obtained through works of love because every good work you do is essential, and it is your salary for a better life.

- But what about those who have hurt others so much but, everything works out in their lives and goes well? People continue to think, and all I can answer is that sooner or later, they will find their way into a blind alley because that is the way for those who love only themselves and hurt each other without understanding that the other is you. Other people are like your mirror, and sooner or later, if you break one, then the life lesson will find you. If you steal someone, the house will burn down in your next life, or the storm will destroy it. Everything that has been done will not be without consequences, even if now it might seem that I will have no results! More important is to focus more on your work and mission, growth, and learn more to do the jobs of truth and love.

A person may make mistakes but, there is an opportunity to learn and learn again to become full of light and enlightened by love.

And yes, love is not only the relationship between two people but, it is described wider and more indescribable. Love is our good deeds; a comforting word said at difficult times, a hand given to rising from difficulties, and a good-natured smile or allotted time, which is especially important on Earth because it is so limited. You never know when your life path can break down in quick and delicate ways. The passage of day and night allows us to realize that this life is limited because we have time to live and time to die.

We must love everything around us and notice beauty in things and beings that we consider unimportant. I like what Felix Dzerzhinsky once said:

- Love is the creator of all good, noble, strong, warm, and bright. -

If you think you are alone, look at the shining stars at night and choose the brightest star from the eternal sky. When you have done it, then you can realize how beautiful and bright it is, and the more you think about it, the more you know that it doesn't shine for no reason and that there is a reason for everything and that there is always a ray of light, that is like hope even in the most challenging moments of life.

If you doubt that some invisible force has created a world order, then look around with ambition and try to see every tiny detail you see in nature and living. Everything is too complicated to have come about by itself. This includes the higher intelligence, which has established all the processes for life to exist in the environment that arose after the incredible explosion.

YOU ARE CREATED AS A CHILD OF LOVE

- I have to tell you, I see through you, I see your way of life. Vincent, you have experienced a lot of suffering and injustice but, the most challenging moment in your life was when your mother disappeared. I see that right now she's sitting on a bench and looking up at the sky, and the warm spring sun warms her face like a gentle caress, comforting her internally, - watching the twilights of darkness, said the holy creature.

- Please, tell me where my mother is? - excited and at the same time sadly asked Vincent.

- Vincent, life had broken her badly, and because of her experiences, the schizophrenia developed, which is why she left you alone and ran away from her home without even wearing shoes. A woman who passed by the church noticed your mother and spoke to her but, she began to yell loudly and wave with her hands, telling her about all sorts of monsters that do not leave her alone! An ambulance was called, and your mother went to care; at that time, social workers also contacted your father but, he wasn't interested in helping you because he was too into his work, so he replied that he had his own family. It is not possible that he has a son outside his family but, later he started to feel guilty, so he finally decided to find you, the pristine man said in a calm tone.

- No, JUST NOT THAT, PLEASE, NO! My dear mummy, I want to see you so much, if only I had known sooner where you are, then you would never have got there, I wouldn't have poisoned myself until the last breath but, I'd be around you now and would take care of you now! I miss you! Please, I pray very much, bring me back to life so that I can correct my mistakes and see my mother's face again and would be able to pull her out of that institution. Just say what do you want in return? I'll do everything! Everything! - The desperate spirit asked as he fell to his knees and prayed loudly.

- No matter how much you wish, I can't bring you back

to life because your body has been dead for several days, - the mystical man sighed.

- But how? I have been here for a short time! - While eyes were wide in amazement, Vincent mused.

- Here, a concept like time doesn't exist because no one gets older and tired, and the day and night aren't changing either. All I can say is that while you're here on Earth, a new spring season will soon begin. Your place is here! After the arduous journey, you can finally relax and settle into your new home, and you will meet your mother but, you have to wait a while, My child, - in a loving voice, determined the mystical creature.

Vincent started to think about what it would be like if he had done things differently. What would have happened if he hadn't drunk and poisoned himself so much on that fateful evening, and if only he had tried harder to find his mother himself, then things would have been different. Still, you can't correct the mistakes anymore, and he wanted to calm himself down with the idea that sooner or later, he would meet his beloved mother.

- I'm ready to wait, - Vincent thought and sat down on the hard asteroid surface, and a warm and cosy joy poured into his heart.

12

If you haven't got anything, you have my love

- Do you want to see your mother? - asked the miraculous being.

- More than anything in the world! The man replied in surprise while was raising his eyes and head.

- Then close your eyes.

As Vincent closed his eyes, small flashes of silver lightning flashed in the middle of the veil of darkness. In front of Vincent's eyes, a white building was surrounded by a birch grove, their branches bent in the wind, and the leaves turned in a peculiar dance. Two women were sitting on a white bench, one with her head down and the other was smiling in the sun, even though her gaze was full of pain. The woman's smile seemed completely unnatural and crooked as if forced.

- Why do you smile all the time? - asked the woman who was sitting next to her.

- I try to feel better, even though I am internally ruined because I don't have any relatives who can visit me. My father and mother have been dead for a long time, and my son has been in a car accident; it hurts internally but, even some evil thoughts can be driven away with a bit of a smile.

A man passed by with his head down while smoking nervously; he approached a woman in a white suit and asked if he could go to the local church because he could only find a little peace there.

At one of the windows of the white house, a long-haired man knocked and loudly said that he wanted to go home. Another shorter man opened the building door and went out into the green yard; socks were put on his hands because he thought they were gloves. The sun in the sky tried to warm the faces of all these people as much as it could but, all around it was felt, like a heavy gray cloud that had fallen on people's minds and prevented them from seeing the beautiful birch leaves or the rays of the sun and songs of the small birds on the branches.

- Thank you for showing my mother's face. I'm glad that she's alive, - Vincent said with tears in his eyes and through a heavy snort, - the only way I recognized her was by her hollow voice. She looked perfect, and it brightened my heart that I could see her face finally.

- Many of these people are depressed and can no longer rejoice in their place in the world because pain and gloomy thoughts have crossed their fragile boundaries, their protective barrier that still kept and hope. People were walking around with their heads down, and negative thoughts, apathy, and inner pain took over the joy of life, and it seemed that life no longer had meaning or value, just pure existence only and following the rhythm of daily life. Separation and loneliness - pain bites, so deep in the heart that it is impossible to weed out tares, even with the strongest hoe, whose roots had stretched, from the first day of the birth because they all weren't expected in this world and a weak childhood experience, which wasn't possible to let go but, most of the people had been in pain for a lifetime.

Even if you don't feel like I'm here to give my hand and love, the key is to continue to stand as a strong mast both during darkness and thunderstorms or on a windless sunny day because no matter what happens, you're strong and don't think you're alone. You always have my love...

- *A storm is an opportunity for pine to show its strength and stability, - Ho Chin Minh once said.*

THE DIFFICULTIES OF LIFE ARE LESSONS THAT MAKE YOU MORE INTELLIGENT AND MORE FULFILLED OF LOVE

All the difficulties that have been in your life have made you the person you are now because the difficult lessons teach you the most. When the creator decided not to be alone and to create the universe, the stars, and Earth, it also knew that there would be evil but still decided to develop it because good cannot be killed; it shall always return to its source from which it is derived.

While it is painful to realize that we have suffered and remembered all the unpleasant memories that life has given to us, at the end of the journey, we can finally rejoice that we have overcome it all, and sooner or later, time will heal all the wounds. If there weren't the slightest difficulties in life, then we would no longer be aware of who we are, and we wouldn't know what the other living being is and that it feels as much as we do because only by feeling on our skin is it possible to open our heart truly.

- A happy life is not about lack of difficulty but, about being able to overcome it, - says writer Helen Adam Keller.

Many injustices arise in life from the lack of accurate and challenging lessons, like salt in the wound that burns like hell, that open our feelings with tears in our eyes to every being in the world, even the tiniest insect.

- Why doesn't the Creator protect us from suffering? Isn't it possible to live without pain? - Vincent asked, frowning.

- Such a life is possible only if there is peace, tolerance, love, help in the world, when we will no longer cause pain to each other and when there will be no more bad thoughts and works but, there is still a long way to go. People can often not control themselves, their thoughts, and their deeds because they repeatedly make the same mistakes. People keep quiet when they should talk or don't act when someone else is in trouble.

Sooner or later, a person goes his own way. After a lifetime, those who have learned from difficulties and become stronger, reach higher levels, and no longer need learning lessons but, those who have gossiped, lied, and been self-centred may initially rest here a little bit. Still, soon as possible, they have to go to Earth again to incarnate in the body of a human or some other living being as it is destined.

What is earned in a lifetime is given back, in the form of body and talents, sometimes these gifts aren't pleasant but, no one is to blame for it, except himself, for harming own aura because everything done good or evil, or how much love is given, creates its world. Nothing slips because everything is written in heaven. We know everything, - whispered the mystical being and put on his head the ancient hood.

Vincent felt that although he was already a grown-up man, he was perceived as a small child in the eyes of a mystical man, and he couldn't understand why it was this way because he wasn't a tiny child neither in its form nor in its form nor number in years. He had already grown up as a man.

- Maybe because internally he is already ancient but, maybe the reason is another? Vincent thought, closing his eyes for a moment.

LIFE IS A GIFT!

There is nothing sadder than non-existence; it is the moment when there is nothing in front of the eyes, no sound, no sight, no touch, no smell, just a moment when you are diving into the vast, lonely darkness. Quiet sleep is so tight but, outside of the dark rest, no matter how strong you want it, it's impossible to break out unless you have hope of the slightest ray, a reason to break away from nothingness.

- If you ask me, does life have a purpose? Then, there is none because life itself is the purpose! Why does Earth is turning? Why is there the sunrise and set? Why is Earth diligently protected by the ozone layer, atmospheres, magnetic fields? Why does human skin have thermoregulatory processes? Why does a snowflake have an asymmetrical, unique, and individual pattern? Yes, it's not without reason but, it's all in the name of life, which is life itself!

The meaning of life is to live, love, be happy and save other lives – more minor and more significant. In life, we learn and overcome the difficulties to become stronger and, albeit more challenging but, ultimately wiser.

There is joy in living and the ability to see miracles like in childhood when there are so many questions and so many miraculous things, phenomena, life is the most beautiful flight, and not even one question arises. What is the meaning of life?

Life is an infinite possibility in infinite variants. Still, its beginning and breakthrough is the most critical moment, though - the small, light bulb broke out of the darkness just like the seed of the plant while it's growing, while persistently and stubbornly it is pushing its little sprout through the heavy Earth. In the exact difficult times, a person breaks out to see the presence of light and a new opportunity, to be born again, and not to be alone, to be with someone, to share and experience love, and to give love to the world with your good works, words, with your life.

- To live means to keep moving forward, - Johnson S.

Seed, soil, root, germ, leaves, flower, fruit - a process that includes the meaning of life and it is living, evolving from the seed, which stores the information inserted by The Creator, and in the right place and time, action to break out to be separated a unit of life, one of all unique and unrepeatable.

There are different moments in life, both full of happiness and full of sadness and sorrow but, despite everything, the ability to live is a gift. Some people feel that life has come as a considerable punishment or torment because you feel like a prisoner in your own body, either it is completely paralyzed, or your legs and arms are not working, or your body is staying still and no matter how much you want to run, or get up from your place. Torment, the disease that destroys the body and with your pain, reminds you every day. I'm here; you will not get rid of me. In those moments of despair, life teaches us to deal with difficulties, to continue to cling to the straw of hope, in the middle of a deep and unfathomable lake because you are alive and just keep your course because the day will come when there will be no more pain or lamentation, no burning sorrow but, only true love and the presence of light, which will heal the deepest and saltiest wounds.

Life is a gift, even if it doesn't seem this way, even if it is difficult to go through it because life has its colors, pale, bright, black, white, red, and yellow - all kinds. After all, it is. Gifts are different but given for the same purpose, to learn but, to eventually learn to love everything from this world because it is all created by the Great Light.

EVERYTHING BAD ONCE ENDS

A bright sphere of light is a vast energy charge with no corners that could pierce and leave large bruises, although life tends to flap its bruises.

The sun, the planet, the human eyes, and atoms are like spheres. Flatly, they resemble a circle but, a ring reminds us that everything in this world has its beginning and end because when one process is circled, the next begins again. Life comes from the Great Light and its forces, and the tremendous energy is inexhaustible. Life is eternal and doesn't end when one life has lived. The most important thing is the path, not the end because when death comes, it is just a transition, just like a butterfly, when it transforms from a tiny larva into a wonderful being with the ability to fly and be free and enjoy the warmth of the Sun on its wings and land on a bright flower in a fragrant meadow on a summer day.

Yes, life is not always a fragrant rose garden because hidden behind the leaves have already sharpened their blades with sharp thorns, ready to protect themselves. Where is the path to a perfect life without pain, hatred, tears, and fear? Can life at all be perfect and without experiencing pain and difficulty? Could a person understand how the other beings feel, give them a helping hand and warm love with a friendly gesture, a smile, help in a difficult moment?

An ideal world would exist if there were more love in the world; for the most part, the word love is perceived as a union of two people but, it doesn't appear only in such a relationship; it is like a crystal clear, pink quartz mist, which includes security, tolerance, peace and in its presence. Then you realize that life has not been lived in vain.

Love is the kind you give - good deeds, words, time, presence, what improves each other's life and makes the soul thaw from the winter frost.

Therefore, life is as it is. It has its horror, which often arises from the loud voice of the Ego or inner fear.

I am that precious and beautiful; look at me but, that one is there below the earth. In this way, many have lost themselves and are far away from the actual source, which is light, love, and forgiveness.

In difficult times in life, it is always essential to love ourselves and each other because we are all created from one material - the beginning and the light. We come from the morning, and we return to the light.

- Life is a way home, - Melville said.

Love is the key to everything and, at the same time, the path to happiness, absolute peace, and fulfilment, without it, the being is like a lost traveller at a crossroads, you don't know where you are but, there are several more paths to choose.

Even if you listen to the voice of your mind, it sometimes whispers wrong because emotions take over. Still, only pure, clear truth and faith in yourself will be able to keep you on your feet as a strong oak trunk even in the strongest storms. Still, when the storms pass, there is always the first ray of sunshine, hope, and a new opportunity because each day is like a small start to a new journey, and the more love you spread around you, the happier you will live it.

- Life has to become, and it can become a relentless joy, - Tolstoy recalls.

Vincent widened his eyes and watched the bright light bulb, which spoke to him in a human voice and reminded him of the shining Sun - the shade of the silver moon. In front of him, the beam of light got closer and closer at high speed, and Vincent was so terrified that he closed his eyelids. At the same time, he felt the love that flowed from the rays of light that shone in various diamond colors - purple, ruby green, transparent sky-blue cloud, purple and soft pink.

- I am the beginning, the light, and the love. I come from the loneliness and the quiet darkness that surrounds everything. At first, I hated darkness because I saw nothing more than that. Still, in time I realized that I have great strength, great energy, and knowledge to move from loneliness to absolute light and grow as an all-encompassing love and remember you are a small part of me but, not at all insignificant. Take a look around yourself! - determined the Sphere of Light.

Vincent's legs were rapidly detached from Earth, and he shot in the air like a magnetic force, just like a swirling geyser, and while he was traveling, he noticed how planets, stars, and asteroids changed their bright glow to dark black. He saw complete darkness all around as if the environment wouldn't have been at all. The dark vaults of skies began to change their shape just like plasticine and were all surrounded by pitch-black matter, a peculiar substance from which everything that arose could just as quickly disappear or be born again.

- This is the key to the universe! The magical substance from which everything is created, you also come from it. Still, the opposites, fire and water, night against the day, moon against sun, negative against positive, arriving and leaving, form the core of light, - determined the voice.

- What does this mean? Is nothing real? - Vincent waved and held out his hand to the gray butterfly, which flew over his palm, and looked at him as if he had met an old friend and blinked kindly with his big eyes while gracefully twitched its wings. The butterfly became a cloud of smoke, which became smaller and smaller until it faded throughout.

- Just like a dream! - In a hollow voice, said Light.

Vincent reached for the nearest ray of the light with the palm of his hand and shuddered deeply when he heard the sound of a sudden flash in the dark horizon of the sky. The bluish, red moments sprinkled like fireworks and illuminated small, black dots in perfect order, forming a vast circle with a white light in the middle.

- This white light is perfect. What is it? - Vincent looked at it and felt how he started to move at a wild speed in its direction.

- No, slower! Please, slower! - Confused, Vincent shouted but, no one answered him.

The speed was so great that everything around it turned into lines of different colors until it merged at one point, in one giant ray of light.

Vincent closed his eyes from the high speed but, when he felt that he was moving more slowly, he opened them wide again and could not believe what he saw. The place he saw looked like Earth, with a white beach and a crystal clear, turquoise sea in front of his eyes. Everything around looked much brighter than usual, and when Vincent turned his head a little, he noticed that the magical and divine ball of light, which had welcomed him so kindly, now had faded and left him in a very, completely strange place, to an unknown planet.

13

The planet of Astra and
its secrets

A white motorcycle was flying out at high speed of the sky edge like a quiet buzz beehive, and as he raised his head, Vincent noticed two thick neon-engraved tires getting closer and closer. The white motorcycle slowly descended slightly, sinking into the white sand. Vincent looked at the beautiful woman sitting at the steering wheel and opened his mouth when he saw her appearance.

- As if human, as if supernatural being. Such a beautiful creature, - Vincent thought.

Her purple, slick bob hair lightly fluttered in the gentle breeze but, her eyes were as big as two buttons, and they were flickering like two green rubies. The nose of the supernatural being was skinny and tiny but, the lips were raspberry pink and diamond-shaped but, her skin color was a little scaly and, from time to time, was gleaming in the sunlight.

- Welcome to your new home, just don't be afraid of me! - in a hollow and velvety tone of voice, the creature said with a smile.

- Who are you? - looking from head to toe, the man asked.

- I am a resident of this planet. My life span is ten thousand years; now I am two thousand years old, I am still very young. I am one of the heavenly beings destined to live longer than the inhabitants of the other planets, and, yes, I am responsible for the spirits who pass to the planet of Astra. You see, my friend! Everything here is entirely different than in your previous world.

- Are we in paradise?

- You can name it as you want! Vincent, I want to show you something!

- How do you know my name? - surprised asked the young man.

- I know enough because I can realize more than you can imagine but, the most fun is to read the thoughts of other people's spirits and beings.

- Are you an alien or a deity? - Vincent asked rapidly.

- No, I am not an alien but, the Light of the universe has endowed me with supernatural qualities, and I am not the only one here like this. Listen, some time ago, I was a human being just like you but, during my life, I sacrificed a lot for others and gave up my Ego and thus pain and suffering; the Great

Light allowed me to be closer to itself while giving a chance to live on this planet. Okay, enough to talk so much because you will soon see everything yourself. Now let's go to the central blockhouse! Please, sit down next to me!

Vincent nodded his head and sat down on the white motorcycle while was watching how it took off slowly with a slight hum. He was a little frightened that he might fall. Still, He realized that nothing would happen anyway because he was no longer alive, even though he felt even more alive than ever, and his excitement could be compared to the first time when he saw Maggie, and his heart began to beat faster.

On the shores of the turquoise blue sea, foamy, white waves floated, and the sea was so crystal clear that one could see through it, even the smallest pebble and the smallest fish which looked in their direction. By the time the two rose high in the skies, there was nothing around, not even a single tree or bush, except the crystal-clear sea and white sand.

The beautiful creature approached the green rocks, all overgrown with ivy leaves, and their sharp peaks sank into the feather bed's soft clouds.

- Hold on tight! - said the creature, and as she turned the handlebars of the motorcycle as a fast elevator, he suddenly descended lower and flew out into the narrow crevice of the rock wall

- Fun! - exclaimed the driver, - We're very close because it's here.

She drove through the ancient gate made of massive stone and recalled the Egyptian pyramid temple, only there was no Egypt or pyramids. The sides of the enormous gates were adorned with various symbols, which shimmered in a chameleon purple color, and when they approached closer, the color changed to heaven blue.

The feminine creature drove out of the gate, and at that moment, a thick fog like a strong wind appeared and pushed both riders back a bit. There was nothing around but a white emptiness but, as the road continued, the veil of fog disappeared and opened a view of white buildings and skyscrapers. A light blue river flowed through the modern high-rise city and glimmered as if it were carved out of gold.

Vincent noticed that the same motorcycles were flown in the skies with whom the mysterious companion was traveling. In the back seats, people were sitting and wearing all kinds of different clothes; one of them looked like he had just stepped out Middle Ages with both feet. The man was overgrown with a long, white beard, and, with one hand, he held a black headdress. The view was comic because he had put on a vest with huge holes in it, which was far too short for him, and he wore black loafers that reminded ballerina's shoes with cords twined to the knees crosswise.

Noticing Vincent, he took off his hat and greeted the travellers with a long sweep and a kind smile. Vincent looked at the creatures sitting on the wheels of the motorcycles and noticed that they all were human-like creatures similar in appearance to both men and women. All of them had purple hairs; only their hairstyle arrangement was various.

For several women, their hair was entangled in small braids

or twisted into large thick dreadlocks but, for men, the hair seemed to be stick to the head with some shiny hair gel. The clothes of the masculine creatures resembled the chef's jackets, which looked quite elegant in a smoky black color and had shiny, metallic rows of buttons on the very front.

Vincent raised his head as he heard the heavy sound of wings fluttering.

- What is it? - Vincent asked and tried to see the silhouette of the great creature in the bright sunlight.

The creature turned towards Vincent and revealed his vampire-like canines with a bit of a smile. Her wings were green, and their surface resembled rock walls.

- She has similar wings like a bat or a bit like some kind of dinosaur-bird but, this creature has a human face, - Vincent said to himself.

- That is some kind of vampire!

- Don't be afraid! She won't bite you! The ally said while laughing and drove closer to the roof of the white building, which looked like a giant sail and landed flatly in the center on top of it. The woman got off the motorcycle and took quick steps in the direction of the elevator, not noticing that Vincent had come very close to the edge of the building and looked at the city landscape, where the green grass reminded of a barely sprouted sprout blanket but, the winding river - bright mirrors that glistened like blue crystals. The floors of the city's buildings glanced like silver in the bright sun but, the sky was covered in purple sheets.

However, although the city was miraculously beautiful and

sprinkled with shiny skyscrapers, still you couldn't feel much life around it, only sometimes, as when some dwellers flew with their modern, nowhere-seen motorcycles.

Vincent's friend stopped and, turning his head like an owl, frowned and shouted:

- Are you coming?

Vincent smiled and followed her while she was watching her white boots. He had never seen such shoes, from time to time on top of them in various colours appeared symbols but, after a while, they disappeared again. As Vincent started to follow his alley, he saw that the elevator in front of him recalled a white mirror shower cabin, speaking in a strange foreign tongue. Still, as its doors opened, the view unfolded a long white hallway with round windows like the deck of a ship.

Vincent noticed that he could have seen a large crowd of human-like laboratory staff creatures behind the windows, all dressed in white coats.

- What's your name? We've been on this trip for a while now but, you haven't told me your name yet.

- Ife! It is an ancient Egyptian name that means love in our language, - said the creature and touched the door chip with the tip of her finger but, with other hand stroked Vincent's shoulder and winked with her eye.

The first thing Vincent noticed when he looked over Ife's shoulder was a man with big, green emerald bright eyes in a white, long shirt, who waved with a broad and kind smile on his face.

- I'm Magnus. Welcome to your new home! How was the trip?

- The best I've had in my life. I had never travelled like this before. This place is perfection itself; only I miss my mother so much because she is extremely far away from me right now.

- Don't worry, you'll meet your loved ones soon! - A man-like creature said and was putting on transparent glasses.

- How do you think? What is this place? - I asked with a smile.

- I think this is a hospital for all broken souls, - Vincent scraped his head and answered.

- I've never heard anything like that before! The Hospital of Broken Souls? Seriously? You're a comedian, Vincent, - the man replied.

- This is a DNA prototyping laboratory. You see, everything is based on DNA information. Human prototypes are created here; other laboratories deal with animal and plant prototypes. Many don't see that everything is pre-planned and more advanced civilizations working for you. Karma is one of the main conditions we consider; for example, sickness is programmed to teach us to become brighter souls in the next life and help overcome the difficulties that make the human spirit much more robust and fuller of love as the Great Light. Sickness and the body's inner and outer shell are all the basis of karma, no matter how we don't want to believe it.

- Does this mean that life on this planet is not eternal?

- Life on this planet is eternal for those who have earned it in a lifetime. Still, for others, life is not infinite and after a while will have to incarnate again in a new form, without re-membering anything from the previous life, and even if some-one would remember, nothing much would change; it would only complicate everything even more because the new family would never be accepted. Still, the family of the previous life and the loved ones would be soughed.

Dear Vincent, one of my abilities is to read people's past lives, and looking through your eyes; I see that you have loved a girl named Maggie very much. She was one of the reasons you turned to addictions, you couldn't accept her rejection anymore, and you were obsessed with her. Vincent, I can ex-plain your obsession quite simply. Firstly, you lacked love as a child, and secondly, you already knew her in a previous life. Yes, it was a long time ago in an earlier life but, you worked at her in the old mill as a servant - poor but overwhelmed with love, and at that time, she was about ten years older than you and didn't even look into your direction because she thought you were a boy. She married an older, wealthier man, she loved him but, he drove her to great ruin. Oh, Vincent, she's like a curse on your shoulders.

I have to say honestly that in this life, we put you both together again in the same village and the same school because the last time we met, you prayed to me on your knees and promised to serve the Great Light to open your heart to help to others and spread your love. Still, unfortunately, you broke your promise because you ended your life with your addic-tions. After all, you were too focused on the negative. Dear Vincent, if you had thought more about the positive, then you would understand that you are always loved, if not there, then here, - the man slapped on Vincent's shoulder and approached the mahogany table, on which stood several glazed glasses. The man took one in his hands and carefully placed them on Vincent's eyes.

Vincent first noticed black-and-white images that turned colorful and rushed through forests and house roofs. The image approached some chimney of a city building, and when the movie in front of him started to fly over the tops it, stopped at people's faces in a paved square of the old town. In the distance, he saw a short metal tower.

- Paris! It's Paris for sure and the old Eiffel Tower! - Vincent exclaimed.

The streets were full of people, and cars flew in the air, recalling big drones but, highways were asphalted and inter-sected in the air like snakes. White box-like, angular carriages moved through them in a quiet hum but, glazed skyscrapers lined next to the long river, and factory buildings had been overgrown with green grass.

Inside one of the skyscraper's glazed windows, which re-minded of a huge mirror, a family sat and ate porridge-like food. A wall deck with a moving projection showed strange hieroglyphs inside the home. The family spoke to each other in a language unheard by Vincent, which sounded a little bit like slow singing but, around the table circled human alike creature that was looking like a robot, or both.

A man came out on the long concrete balcony in a white, motorcyclist-like leather jacket. He smiled broadly while was looking into the distance as if dreaming of something; a vast spaceship was gliding over the roof of the building at that moment. The man's eyes followed the giant machine like a magnet but, by the time the aircraft flew away, it disappeared into the white clouds.

The glazed sunglasses became transparent, and through them, one could see the smiling man sitting at his massive table like a boss.

- How did you like the small insight into the future? - the man asked.

- I'm a little stunned by everything that's going on here. I would be more interested in what awaits me soon in a short time! - Vincent replied.

- Time? Time does not exist here, just like many things in the world, doesn't exist at all! Time is an artificial division of the dial that divides action but, the main reference points are birth and death, and everything in the middle is life. Life is what you should think about! You just saw human life after many years, as long as humanity survives that long.

- What do you mean by that? Vincent asked quietly.

- For people to survive in the future, they must learn to give up hatred and become friendlier to each other, especially to Mother Nature. In the ideal future, the city will coexist with nature and people will no longer eat meat, and many jobs will be replaced because of rapid technological change by robots. Still, people will spend more time with their families, break down the language barriers and finally speak in one language without wars and massive conflicts. The duration of a lifetime will increase. Still, it will never be possible to obtain immortality because it is only possible for the elect.

- A distant future doesn't bind me; if I can't return to life now, then I don't want to go back to life ever!

- It's not possible! You have to build a better world, just like everyone else.

- Why? Why can't I live in peace forever if I am already dead? So then, where is this paradise? - Vincent asked and put his sunglasses on the table.

- You have to look for paradise in your heart because it has the answers to all the questions. You had made a huge mistake when you decided to commit suicide, yet many had done suffer and pain to you but, you still found forgiveness, so you have earned to be here in paradise, or how you people call it.

- Ife, where did you go, please come back? - the man asked and turned on an unusual blue laser projection through which it was possible to see the features of a beautiful woman's face.

Vincent got a bit scared when they heard a sudden knocking on the window. Ife winked with one eye and shrugged her head toward his side.

- She likes surprises! Haha! - The man laughed.

Vincent came closer to the window and felt how the wind passed through his whole body.

- You feel alive again, right? Get on top!

As he looked down, Vincent touched the large window's glass and felt how its hard surface had changed and had become an empty air. Ife held out her hand, and Vincent stared into her smoky green eyes, immersing into them like in sinking sand, while he didn't even notice how he was already sitting next to her.

In a calm silence, they flew over the glowing skyscrapers of the buildings, which wore various colours as the sun shone.

- How beautiful everything looks from the view of a bird's eye. I would never get tired of flying around just to watch such a beauty, - Vincent thought.

The wind touched his face lightly, and the crystal-bright rays of the sun went through his whole airy body, and Vincent felt as much joy and happiness in his heart as the memories of his mother, how she used to hug him or with her smile warmed the darkest and saddest corners of his heart. He sensed elevating feeling just like he had met the beautiful girl, Maggie, for the first time. Now, he felt as happy as in all the short happy moments he had felt on Earth.

Ife descended very close to the winding river with a giant leap, which restlessly rippled when the motorcycle approached its surface. When they passed a brown gondola, Vincent saw a long tall silhouette rowing in front of them. He wanted to look into his face but, he couldn't see the slightest facial feature of a being's face under his wide hood.

Vincent tried to reach for his hood with his hand, and he managed to tear it off with a slight bend.

- It is impossible! This creature looks like an ordinary black shadow or dark silhouette; there is no face, nothing.

- I wouldn't do it if I were you. The sailors can get easily annoyed; they tend to get quite angry if you cross the line, they don't talk much but, they also have feelings, - Ife looked at Vincent with her big button eyes and frowned a bit.

The black silhouette turned to Vincent's side and, with a sharp gesture, snatched the oars of a wooden boat, pulling a massive ball of water out of the sea, and started moving it in a circular motion, in the direction of both travellers.

Vincent opened his mouth to yell that Ife had to fly aside but, it was too late, and the big ball had melted against the side hull, and the motorcycle turned in a slight whirl.

14

My new home

- What a familiar place! - Vincent thought while was looking at the picturesque view with green hills resembling soft green goose feathers. The little river and the old wooden mill, dancing with the wind, turned in a quiet and special dance. A little further down the stone-paved road, a white house stood tall, and small birds with yellow bellies chimed on its balcony that he had never seen before.

Ife landed on a perfectly smooth road, and Vincent realized he had come home. Ife tapped Vincent on his shoulder and said with a warm smile:

- Our road is over. Behold, this is your new home!

- But wait, where are you going? I don't know anyone here. I'm entirely alone!

- You have people waiting for you at home, - Ife winked and sat back on the motorcycle.

- I'm left alone again! - Vincent thought and watched how Ife started the engine of the heavy iron motorcycle and rose high in the air with a murmur and flew at tremendous speed to the town of skyscrapers in the distance, the high floors of which were visible, over the light ruby green hills.

A little bee perched on Vincent's arm and looked with his little eyes and flew away to the small beehive, followed by a whole army of bees, the sane of which resembled a beautiful symphony - Mozart or Bach.

Vincent pulled the wooden door and saw that several young people were sitting in the middle of the room at the massive table, which had been covered with a large tablecloth and a variety of foods. He felt that they all were full of warmth because of their kind-hearted smiles.

- We were waiting for you, even though it wasn't your time yet, - said a beautiful woman who had the same hair and eye color as Vincent.

- You don't know me but, I had always been apprehensive and overwhelmed by you and your mom - my dear daughter! Vincent, I'm your grandmother and love you very much, my little sunshine! Come to me; I have wanted to hug you for so long!

- Wait, are you my grandmother but, how can you be so young? - Vincent asked in amazement as he got closer.

- This place makes the old one new again. Everyone can be accessible in the heart and free from all the shackles of pain!

Vincent, I haven't told you my name yet! My name is Liz, and your brother is sitting here at the table. We call him Tobias; however, his mother didn't give a name to him.

- Call me, just Tobi, - the tall man said with a big smile.

- Wait but, I don't have a brother!

- Yes, you have; I'm even standing here in all my essence!

- I don't understand anything.

- Don't worry, I see by your eyes that you're very thrilled. Look, I had to come into the world five years earlier than you. Still, it was that I missed the moment of the arrival of my soul because I wasn't ready yet. My life was withdrawn, and also it happened because our mom started having health problems, and quite simply, I stayed here and was waiting for you because my second chance to learn and gain experience will be together with you.

- What are you talking about?

- Time here is not eternal, and sooner or later, we all have to return to Earth; only the beings who have reached a great degree of maturity of the soul can remain here altogether. The laws of karma that we record in our lifetime result from everything we have done but, the consequence is what we have to experience to learn and clean the dirt of our soul, which pushes us away from the Great Light. Yes, I know that I have often acted wrong in my previous lives. I was thinking only of myself, and I had caused pain to other people, so this pain called me back to correct everything as a completely different person.

- Wait, I want to know more! - Vincent looked into the man's dark eyes as he put his hand on his arm.

- Enough to talk about such serious topics. Vincent, we're not all familiar with you! My name is Christine, I'm your mom's sister but, I'm younger than you right now. Haha, - Vincent heard silvery laughter like the creaking leaves of a birch on a spring day that was winding through the air.

- I'm Harald, your father's brother, I went into this sun earlier than I had planned but, I'm glad we met! You see, you're not alone, as you had felt so many times because you have a whole circle of supporters!

- I'm your mom's sister's husband, David! Nice to meet you! - said the tall and massive physique young man.

- You all look so young, maybe thirty years old but not more. I am also happy to meet you all, and I am glad that I am not alone. It's such a joy! I have so much to find out about this place, even though it looks like on the planet Earth but, I feel like a completely different place. I am happy here for no reason, and peace and happiness flow into my heart but, one thought overwhelms me. How can I help my mom? I didn't know where she was for so many years, which drove me into ruin. I think that was why I started to drink alcohol to forget a little bit.

- Unfortunately, life played its cards, and her spirit broke when Tobias died, and soon, she fell into severe depression. Your father knew all about it but, the love between the two had vanished, and he had gotten into his work too much but, years later, they met again, and a short romance was formed, even though he already had a wife and then you were born. Mom was thrilled that you were born but, at the same time, she felt unfortunate and because she couldn't let go of her thoughts on the past. Your mom often thought of her heavy childhood. As wicked nightmare memories of her aggressive father often came alive, who used to beat her when he had drunk his point once again but, most of all, she couldn't forget the loss of her baby. Now, she has erased all these memories, just sometimes she is crying out for your name but, don't worry, she's doing well because she is well cared for by the nurses, and she also has a couple of friends there but, she doesn't remember much and her mind is darkened. Vincent, when the time comes, you'll meet her but, until then, we can't do anything because we're too far apart away.

- Come with me! I want to show you something! - Said Tobias and passed through the sizeable ivy-covered door

- I want you to come with me to the big mill, - Tobias said with glowing eyes.

They walked along a narrow pebbly path, and Vincent saw the bright roses and daisies moving in the wind as if they were very much alive. Bees were quietly buzzing at their petals and were dancing from one flower to the other but, when they got closer, they flew towards the windmill.

Tobias pushed the bolted massive doors with a sharp hand gesture and jumped up on the white stone stairs in a quick step. Vincent heard a loud squeak of the jamb and the sound of a quiet door knock as if it was talking. When he came closer to the mill ridge, he noticed a door at the end of the ladder with a round crystal-like handle, he turned it, and the first thing he saw was Tobias's head and how he was pressing against the small window.

- Vincent, take a look! This is a special place. I want you to take a closer view. Come on, faster!

Vincent looked outside the window and noticed that the surrounding of the green meadows and snoring streams were being replaced with an unfamiliar place. Bushy spruce tops and a white sanatorium appeared in front of his eyes, and in one of the windows, he could see the woman's silhouette.

- That's my mother, she's got very grey hair but, there are no wrinkles on her face. I love her smile while she looks at the little sparrows that are knocking on the windowpane.

- You see, Vincent, she's fine! Above all, send her good thoughts and wishes, then joy and happiness will pour into her heart so that she is as fortunate as when you first entered the world and when she put you on your breast.

- You could be a poet!

- Remember, I could have been your brother, and even though it wasn't easy for you, I would have helped you to deal with all the difficulties. Look further! Mills' likes to talk when there's something to say!

Vincent narrowed his eyes to the flicker of colors. When he was opening them again, he noticed that a red sun rose through the window in the distance, painted the purple color in the skies, and illuminated the fields of cultivated ground. On the field's horizon, two farmers were running at a fast pace with wicker baskets in their hands. They both were so fast that these men's faces appeared in the window in a short time. Vincent slipped from his fright and fell on his back with his mouth wide open while looking at their faces.

- Hahaha! - Tobias laughed deliciously, - don't be afraid, these people are us, just some two hundred years ago, we were brothers back then. Although time is not counted here, I've spent a lot of time here because here you never stay old and you're always full of energy.

Vincent stood up and quickly jumped to the small window and opened it and pulled out his hand but, at the exact moment, all the silhouettes disappeared as if they had never existed.

- What's this place?

- This whole place is magical and incomprehensible. I have spent a lot of time here while I was waiting for you all but, there is still a lot of undiscovered. This place hides many secrets but, only to protect us.

- What are you talking about? This whole new world is perfect!

- By this, I mean that the mill tries to protect us from ourselves and life on Earth, which lies ahead because it's always silent about the future. Unfortunately, we know nothing and it is a bit scary.

- Yes but, what is this weird mill? - Vincent asked.

- This is a way to communicate with the Big Light and know more about yourself. Maybe you don't remember me from a previous life right now but, I remember you because we were always like best friends, standing for each other and falling. Vincent, don't you remember us? We fell in love with the same girl at that time, she was the reason why our paths separated and why we got in such vast conflicts that we didn't talk to each other for several years but, you couldn't leave her and stayed near her as a servant for all your life.

- I'm sorry but, I don't remember anything! - Vincent looked at Tobias in a deep puzzlement towards the window of the mill and hoped to see its story again.

- How can one girl twist men's heads like this? The story started when we started to work on her farm manor as stable boys. I still remember the first time I saw her riding on a white horse, her long golden hair shone in the sun's rays, and I immediately fell in love with her like a fool. I have to say that she was the most beautiful woman I had ever seen and the first time she came up to me, I felt so embarrassed that I couldn't make a sound out of my mouth because I didn't even hear, what she was saying to me, I could only feel the smell of her meadow flowers, which she held in her gentle hands. Her blue eyes reminded me of two crystals whose brilliance could break into any heart. At least with both of us, it had happened. I always tried to show her attention, tried to be near her, and often observed her through the windows. My heart broke every time she spoke to you and responded with a smile; in those moments, I always thought she was flirting with you, and I was so angry inside that I wanted to run up to you and strike you hard, so you don't forget. I always thought she paid more attention to you than to me but, the most painful thing was that she married that old rich clown, who was so arrogant and ugly. The most incomprehensible thing was that she really loved him but, he often had other women by his side while she waited patiently at home.

- And what happened next? Why are you telling me this? - Vincent stared in surprise at Tobias's face.

- I told Emily about the two other women with whom her husband had a romance, then she burst into tears and I tried to kiss her but, she pushed me away, and she got on her knees in the corner of the room and cried hysterically. I realized that I wouldn't fight for her love anymore, and I'd instead go somewhere far away and, best of all, if someone shot me to end this suffering. I decided to go to the army but you stayed as a servant boy.

Yes, time heals wounds, and I forgot about her and met another girl little by little but, you continued to be around her as obsessed. Vincent, this girl is the same Maggie you're still in love with, and all your love for her has overshadowed your memories of your previous life, so I came here with you, so you remember our old story. I am so sorry that one girl distorted our heads so much that our relationships ended. Still, now we have another opportunity to rebuild our relationships, and I hope that we will meet again soon, - said Tobias and lowered his head.

- What are you talking about? Are you going somewhere? This place is timeless.

- Now that you are here, I must go back to Earth, that is the rule, and I don't mind.

- But wait, who is even making all these rules?

Vincent, I know very well that you've just come here, and you have a lot of unanswered questions, so if you want, we can go to skyscraper city together, - Tobias said with a smile.

A drop of tears fell to Tobias's cheeks, and as he hugged Vincent, he realized he might never meet him again. Vincent tried to solace him but, he didn't seem to listen to him at all. He said he would feel much better if Vincent went to Earth with him but would understand if he didn't want to.

It wasn't long before the creature seen before - a silhouette without a face and with a wide hood - oared at the shore of the small stream. Both men climbed into the gondola and started to sail along the winding creek, and while on the trip, they saw many different animals running happily through the meadows. At one point, three caramel-colored horses with long mane were running with them near the coastline; they seemed to greet and kindly accompany them on the way.

Vincent especially remembered the big oak; on whose thick branch a creature was sitting. The mystical creature had wings resembling a bat but, its surface was like a dinosaur era - green, shiny, scaly color. The beast had a female body but, only the wings made her different.

When the creature had noticed the travellers, she flew away over their heads. She looked at Tobias and giggled as if knowing something and exposed her sharp tusk teeth, which resembled a vampire. This beautiful creature was similar to Ife and seeing her; Vincent hoped to meet his friend, with whom he had so many good memories when they had ridden a motorcycle.

Vincent started to think about Ife and remembered that she looked like a goddess or being who got out of a fairy tale book. Still, unfortunately, he didn't meet her in the place where Ife had brought him for the first time, to the same smiling man who always sat in his spacious and glazed office.

The man with the white coat showed him several laboratories and explained that they were working here with the latest technologies that have not yet been invented on the human planet and showed us some diagrams and codes of DNA. He also said that DNA is the central core of everything.

Vincent remembered what he said:

- Even before we are born, DNA encodes the primary information, how we will look in the future, what diseases are expected, and even how many years human beings will live. The skies can record human and all alive beings' lives as in film, and always remember that the essential thing in life is giving love and having peace in the heart.

The man warned Tobias that he would face difficult trials but, he must stay strong and take everything as a life lesson and not as a punishment.

Tobias could choose what color he wanted eye and hair color. The man in the white suit even showed what he would look like when he grew up. Vincent started to laugh at the moment when Tobias began arguing with a lab worker that he didn't want to have yellow teeth. Still, the woman said she couldn't help him because his parents didn't have adequate DNA and that he should be glad that he is going to have a body at all because so many people's spirits want to go to Earth but, they have to wait for their row.

Tobias was deeply frightened when he realized that he was about to go to another place, and he began to ask all sorts of questions:

- How much time will it take to be able to go back here? What awaits me on Earth? When I sleep nine months in my mother's belly, won't I suffocate? And will I remember at least something when I will be on Earth, and how will I know about all of you and the Great Light?

The muscular man looked quite tired from all these questions and just answered:

- You'll know about the Great Light when you will arrive on Earth but, now it's time to go.

Vincent was amazed when he walked with Tobias into a white and empty room with a white slide in the corner of the room, which went so far away that the end was not visible. One last time, Tobias tapped Vincent on the shoulder, and they hugged as he whispered in his ear:

- I'm scared but, I hope I will see you soon at the other end. This man promised me that we would be brothers, and hopefully, it would stay this way.

The moment he left the place, Vincent felt a deep pain in his heart; strangely, it seemed that a small fraction had deserted him. There were too many unanswered questions in Vincent's mind, so he decided not to wait for Ife to go back to his cozy mill home but, instead, he ran into the elevator to see every floor of the building and every corner of its rooms. What he saw surprised him...

In one of the rooms he entered, there was a view of white snow-capped mountains, white snowflakes were swirling all around, and he felt again as a child, as the first time when a small snowflake had fallen into his hand. The little heart began to beat faster because it seemed like a small gift, and he couldn't understand who could create such a work of art? The moment he turned his head back, Vincent saw a retros-style dark green car that was coming after him. He realized he had come to a secret, so he kept running towards the spruce forest and went to a wooden house. Vincent reached out to the door handle, and from behind, someone shouted:

- Stop, where are you running?

But he didn't want to stop, and he hastily opened the moss-covered doors.

The comfortable wooden house reminded me of his child-hood home; it had completely different furniture. He noticed some known woman who sat at the table and read the book. Vincent walked close to her with as quiet steps as possible to see what she was reading. She turned her head in his direction. The fear appeared in the woman's big eyes, and she tried to scream but couldn't make a sound. The dark-haired girl ran out of the room but, on the way, her foot caught on behind the porch, and she fell to the ground. Vincent tried to come closer to help her get up but, his hand went through the woman's pale arm as he had become a transparent, silver silhouette of clouds. As soon as the beautiful woman stood up, she ran away without looking back at the speed of the wings of the wind but, a short time later, the long-haired man Vincent had seen previously appeared in the door gap. A little farther away between thick snowdrifts, his car was silently growling.

- This place is like thin ice between two worlds - between Earth and here. Everyone will find a different location here but, it will always take you to the deepest parts of your broken heart. The girl was terrified of you because she saw your spirit, and next time, please don't disturb her because, without unnecessary, there is no need to crawl into the people's world. Vincent, you have a new life now! Please find peace!

Vincent noticed a silver light coming out of the man's heart. Unable to utter a word, he ran out of the tiny house and obsessively looked around, hoping to see a girl he hadn't seen for so long.

Vincent, it's not love but obsession; you have to leave her alone finally!

- I can't. I can't just let her go so quickly. I thought I'd forget her if I died but, I still can't! My new home is here, and I don't want to go anywhere else! I'll stay here and wait for her to come back.

- You know, it's not allowed to interfere in human life. This portal isn't meant to be this way. Vincent, you must leave her alone, and also, you've recently died, so your dense spirit is also visible to people.

- Then please give me wings! I know you are a superhuman being and the supreme power. Please, allow me to become her guardian angel!

15

Time to leave

A LETTER TO MAGGIE!

Hi, I want to tell you that I am thinking about you and miss you so much. I miss your smile, your crystal-deep glowing eyes; looking at them, I drown like in the ocean every single time, and I miss your thick heather-scented hair. If you would know, how many times have I wanted to touch them? But I've never dared to.

Maggie, even though we didn't manage to be together and even though I wanted it more than anything in the world, I have to tell you I'm dead right now but, still alive, and still I can't get you out of my mind.

This place where I am now is like a fairy tale; it seems that this place is not accurate but, more like a dream, and still, I can't believe that this is not a dream but, is a reality - a real place in a different dimension, without any time limits but, full of love.

Most importantly, I found a place that can lead to your soul's greatest desires, and this place is your heart and my memories, which created an invisible path, a portal to you.

I am grateful for the time I spent in your presence. I had the opportunity to be with you without you even realizing it because I became your guardian angel but, now it's time to let you go, and it's so hard for me...

Maggie, no matter how much my heart hurts, I want you to be happy but, now it's time for me to return to Earth to be born in a new body again. I hope you will find and read this letter that comes from the bottom of my heart to the only love of my life, and I hope that one day I will meet you again and see your beautiful smile and your deep, big eyes, in which I see the whole world.

I want you to know that there is something more than just living life on Earth and that after death, everything continues because nothing can die.

My Maggie here is peace, and I finally feel filled with happiness and love internally, so never worry in your life because there are invisible forces that love you and protect you but, most of all, I am thinking about you always...

Your guardian angel
Vincent

Vincent folded the letter into several parts and placed it on the heavy, grayish desk and watched as a wooden door opened with a small, shrill squeak and a white light shone through the tiny gap but, when the door's spread a little more, the first thing Vincent noticed was the dark, brown, curly hair.

- It's you! I remember you very well from the time you had chased me with your green car but, I already know what you're going to tell me because I feel it in my heart.

- It's time to go, Vincent! - the tall man said and pointed his hand at the door from which Vincent had once entered the wintering world and had found the way that had led him to the mysterious wooden house. Standing in front of the man, from whom the golden light radiated, he couldn't stop thinking about Maggie and that he might never see her again. Vincent began to breathe faster and decided to stay here and go anywhere despite everything.

- I don't want to go to Earth!

- You have to go! - the man growled.

- Please, I can't leave. She's all I need. She's like the air I need to be able to breathe. Only she fills my heart and I see no point in my existence without her. Do you realize that I want to be close to her constantly and protect her? Please, give me a chance to stay here because if I have to go back to Earth now, I won't be in her age anymore. Give me a single chance to wait for her in this place, and then I'm ready to go back wherever you say.

- No, you have to go! Your time has come!

Vincent went to the small kitchen one last time and stared at Maggie with a pain in his eyes while she was gazing into the scenic ice flowers of the windowpane and touched them with her fingers its winding flowers. If only she knew that these flowers were a painting of Vincent, which he drew while she slept under a warm blanket with another man.

Vincent stroked her hair and kissed her lips. She felt a cold touch like a caress of wind while he wiped her lips and touched her back of the head.

- I hope that one day I will meet you again, if not on Earth, then at least here in this place, when I come back from the world's roads, and I hope you will find and read my letter. Maggie, if only I could bring back time, I would have tried harder to be with you when I was still alive. I would have tried my best then. I would have sent you more of my poems and roses every day, just to get your attention, even the slightest moment with you, or to see your beautiful eyes. Indeed, your eyes mean everything to me, as so does your warm smile. I'm going to miss you so much! - When Vincent said that, he felt how his feet rose half a meter above the ground and started to fly at tremendous speed with magnetic force. Vincent made his way through the same path he had come, and as if time had been turned back, he flew through the snowy forest trail and stared at the swirling snowflakes that landed in thick snow-drifts that glittered like hidden tiny diamonds in the sun.

- I'm so worried because I don't know what's waiting for me, - Vincent quietly determined and tilted his head while he was watching to all body and slipped to the same room where once stood, Tobias

Vincent felt that his body was sliding into a white tunnel, to whom he couldn't see the end. He closed his eyes and glided through a white light gently surrounded by a thick fog while he could no longer see himself. Vincent closed his eyes because the bright light was suddenly replaced by pitch-black darkness, it was only briefly but, as he continued his way, the world opened like a beautiful gem in front of his eyes. Earth was dark blue, and there had a view of its green silhouettes of continents, which he approached closer and closer at more incredible speed. Vincent flew through the thick cumulus, and the first thing he saw was the dense pine forest layouts that had surrounded by a wavy sea of white foam, washing the golden sandbanks.

Vincent saw the roof of a white building shining through the forest, and as he flew closer, he discerned a young woman standing by the window. She was about to go to work and searched for the car keys but, when she finally found them fallen behind the wardrobe, she got a headache and nausea.

Vincent was no longer Vincent because he no longer had his old name, and he didn't have his ancient past. Instead, he was greeted by a whole new life. His little heart was beating, and when he took a deep breath, he felt that he was alive again and felt his mother's warmth. The baby opened his little mouth and smiled. It was very dark but comfortable enough to turn slightly from side to side.

The young woman put both hands crosswise on her stomach and asked:

- How do I name you? Hmm... Maybe Marcus but, if you're a girl, then Jasmine? I want you to know that I'm going to love you, whether you're a girl or a boy, - a woman smiled and gently stroked her stomach.

Ten years later

- Mom, look at my drawing!

- How beautiful! You have drawn a big beautiful house, and I love the long green spruces around the house. You're a real artist.

- Look! - The boy said, - and the neighbor's orange cat is lying on the stairs.

- But honey, our neighbors don't have an orange cat.

- It's not our neighbor's cat. It's a cat from my previous life, like this house I had drawn, - the boy put the colored pencils in a canister and pointed his finger at the little cat.

- I don't know where you learned to draw like this but, I think you should go to Art School because you're a real artist and have such a rich fantasy.

- Mom, I'm telling the truth! It's not a fantasy or a dream I have seen. Mom, that's true.

- Did you do your homework or not?

- We didn't have homework today. Mom, please listen because I have so much to tell you about but most of all I'd like to go back to my old house again, and I would like to see my previous mom.

- Well, you're talking nonsense because I'm your real and only mom.

- Mom, I'm begging you, we should go to my previous home, which I still remember. Yes, my memories are clouded but, I know that my mom had brown, long hair and brown eyes. We both had lived together in poor conditions because I remember that the house walls were covered with grey mold, and I was wearing a torn, dirty shirt. We often had nothing to eat because the fridge was empty, and I tried opening it again and again, hoping that food would appear. I also remember playing with the fat neighbor's cat Murki.

- Tell me, honey, where's this house?

- I remember living in a two-floor house with windows like dwarf huts, and they were bolted with wooden slabs that were green as salads. I see in front of my eyes that the ancient house is built of wooden boards but next to the house, there is a spruce forest, and in the yard stands a pantry building built of stones. Mom, I still remember the way to my home village, and I see a white sign written with black letters on the road - Burley. I see all of this sometimes in my dreams and some-times when I close my eyes, and I know very well that this is true and there is no fantasy, - the youngster determined with his eyes closed and sighed quietly.

- Okay, what else do you remember? - Mom looked at her son with big eyes.

- I remember that my name used to be Vincent and that I had orange hair just like my neighbor's cat, although it's strange that I now have black curly hair. I have to say that I am trying very hard to remember what my mom's name was from a previous life but, nothing comes to mind, all I remember is that my mom's relative's name was Eva. Mom but that's not the only thing because I remember not only my previous life, I also remember when I was dead but, at the same time, I felt more alive than ever, and also I remember being madly in love with a girl with dark hair but, I don't remember what her face looked like.

Mom chuckled and pulled out a transparent umbrella from underneath the closet:

- It always falls behind the thick winter sweaters.

- I think it will rain a little bit outside but, it will go away quickly.

- I will be soon ready. I already wore the rubber boots, - with small quick steps, the little boy was already outside of the house and reached the glassed front door as he jumped with two giant steps.

- Come on, Mom, come on! I want to be on time for the carousels because they will close soon.

Warm and summery rain hit her mom's face, and she made such a facial gesture as if she had eaten a sour lemon. The painted mascara slowly slid over her cheeks and resembled two black streams.

- Well, how do I look now? We have to go back home. I can't show up anywhere like that.

- No, Mom, I have one napkin in my pocket. Wipe your eyes, and let's go to the carousels!

Crossing the city's cobbled square, white flying carousel's swans appeared in front of both eyes. Between the green maple tops, colorful silhouettes of people sat inside of them, and one of them was vigorously waving.

- Mom, I want to go to that carousel with the light blue swan that flies the highest.

- No, you're too small! You're going to start crying. Let's go to drive with electric cars!

Mom got a little scared when a woman put her hand on her shoulder. The woman looked like an artist or poet because she had dressed in bright speckled clothes, and her long skirt slightly fluttered in the wind. The slender woman was smiling with such a big smile that her eyes looked a little shut down but, they flashed like two lake crystals through the tiny gaps.

- Hi, I almost didn't recognize you. I guess you've become rich!

- Wow, it's nice to see you here. What's new in your life?

The artistic woman already opened her mouth and wanted to say something when little Marcus pulled his mom's sleeve and said with his eyes spread out.

- Mom, I want to ride with a flying swan!

- Well, I don't know you're still too young.

- But I am ten years old!

Marcus saw that a young and sympathetic guy with soft strands of hair and a red t-shirt with a mill printed on top of it held with his both hands ice cream cones tightly clenched with green balls on top of them. He quickly approached from the side of the ice cream stand, and the smiling young man came very close to the artistic woman and offered one of the ice creams.

- I told you I didn't want to eat ice cream, - she said through clenched teeth.

- That is my son, always running around!

The guy leaned closer to Marcus and offered the green ice cream.

- Where have I seen him? I can't understand but, he reminds me of somebody, especially his hyperactivity. I feel like he has so much energy that he can't stand still, - the boy thought while was looking directly into his eyes.

- Maybe you want to ride together with him in the blue swan? - mom asked and squatted while he fitted his shirt collar.

- Yes, of course! No problem! I will tell the man sitting at the remote so that he doesn't let the swan fly too high, - He smiled at the boy and went to the ticket stand, which reminded a massive mushroom with a red hat.

The guy vigorously pulled his student card out of his pocket with such a gesture that he hit with his elbow the man standing behind him, who angrily, said something.

- Hey, will you show me your card? I want to see your picture.

The man handed the card to the little boy and looked surprised. Marcus put the card very close to his face and couldn't believe what he had read.

- It says, Tobias Meyer? Tobias? Your name is Tobias! So that's why I thought I had met you somewhere before! We're familiar! We are brothers! - Marcus said aloud and noticed the people in the back were turning their heads in his direction.

- If only you knew how happy I am to see you! Marcus hugged Tobias so tightly that he seemed to break slightly and looked high into the sky at the flying swans, who slowly glided towards the warm evening sun.

www.ingramcontent.com/pod-product-compliance
Lightning Source LLC
LaVergne TN
LVHW020740200726
843506LV00009B/832